HUNDRED CHART

Here's a convenient way to visualize natural numbers from 1 [...] into 10 rows, with 10 numbers in each row.

You might want to make several copies of this chart (or print some from the internet). Then you can experiment with number patterns. For example, color in all the multiples of 4 and see what patterns appear. Or make the multiples of 3 one color and the multiples of 5 another color. What will you do when you get to 15? What other ideas can you think of? How about coloring in all the prime numbers or all the Fibonacci numbers?

1	2	3	4	5	6	7	8	9	10
11	12	13	14	15	16	17	18	19	20
21	22	23	24	25	26	27	28	29	30
31	32	33	34	35	36	37	38	39	40
41	42	43	44	45	46	47	48	49	50
51	52	53	54	55	56	57	58	59	60
61	62	63	64	65	66	67	68	69	70
71	72	73	74	75	76	77	78	79	80
81	82	83	84	85	86	87	88	89	90
91	92	93	94	95	96	97	98	99	100

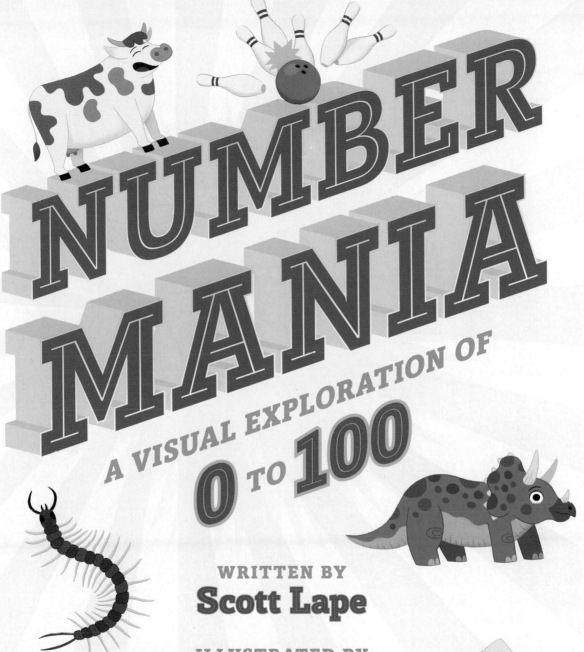

NUMBER MANIA

A VISUAL EXPLORATION OF 0 TO 100

WRITTEN BY
Scott Lape

ILLUSTRATED BY
Víctor Medina

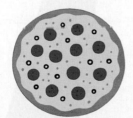

odd dot

NEW YORK

To Mom and Dad —S. L.

Dedicated to number eleven —V. M.

Joyful Books for Curious Minds

An imprint of Macmillan Children's Publishing Group, LLC
Odd Dot® is a registered trademark of Macmillan Publishing Group, LLC
120 Broadway, New York, NY 10271 • OddDot.com • mackids.com

EDITOR Kate Avino
DESIGNER Tim Hall
PRODUCTION EDITORS Hayley O'Brion & Jennifer Healey
PRODUCTION MANAGER Jocelyn O'Dowd

ISBN 978-1-250-90304-4
Library of Congress Control Number 2023057508

Our books may be purchased in bulk for promotional, educational, or
business use. Please contact your local bookseller or the Macmillan
Corporate and Premium Sales Department at (800) 221-7945 ext. 5442
or by email at MacmillanSpecialMarkets@macmillan.com.

First edition, 2024
Printed in China by Dream Colour (Hong Kong) Printing Limited, Guangdong Province
10 9 8 7 6 5 4 3 2 1

Welcome to
NUMBERMANIA!

This book tells you all about the numbers from 0 to 100 through thousands of facts. Numbers go on forever, of course, but that would make this a very long book!

If you like numbers, you will *love* this book. Each section will give you lots of fascinating facts about one particular number. For example, did you know that not only is 16 a square number, but there are also two towns called Sixteen? Or that human spines have 33 bones? And if you think numbers are boring, you're in for a surprise! Numbers are not just the answers to addition problems—they all have their own personalities. Read this book and get to know them better!

But what *is* a number? It might seem like a silly question, but if you think about it, numbers *are* rather mysterious. What is a Seven? We usually write it as 7, but that's just a *numeral*, a symbol that stands for a number. There are other numerals that can represent Seven: In Roman numerals, it's VII, and in Chinese numerals, it's 七. And *seven* is just its name in English; every language has a different word for it.

To understand a number like Seven, we might look at some pictures:

Each group shown above has 7 objects in it. The groups contain very different types of objects, but they have something in common: their *number*. The number Seven is that quality of "sevenness" that all groups of 7 share. You can't touch a Seven—it's not a physical thing—but it exists, somehow. Numbers are mysterious and slippery, but they are also useful and interesting and even . . . beautiful.

NUMBERS AROUND US

If you look around, you see numbers—technically, numerals—everywhere. You see them on vehicle license plates, in phone numbers on billboards, and on street signs. They're used to show time on digital clocks, to show the channel you're watching on TV, and to tell you which bus or train to take. And of course, you see them in math class!

Departures

Time	Bus
06:57	71
07:01	80
07:08	60

West 36th St

Labels

In many cases, numerals are used as nothing more than labels. For example, a car's license plate number is just a label that identifies that vehicle; a license plate of ABC 852 doesn't mean that the car has 852 tires. But numbers used as labels are still very interesting. If you grow up riding the number 41 bus, you'll always have a soft spot in your heart for that number; if you live in apartment number 77, you'll always notice a double 7 when it shows up.

Measurements

Very often, the numerals we see are measurements, and these truly can be called numbers because they refer to a certain number of units. A snake might have a length of 24 inches, and a walk

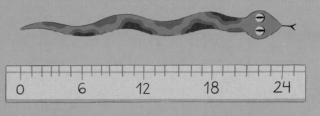

around the block might take 30 minutes of your time. It's important to realize that the numerical value of a measurement depends on the unit that's used: For example, a length of 24 inches can also be expressed as 2 feet. That's why we always include the units—dollars, hours, inches, etc.—when we describe a measurement.

Counting Numbers

Other numerals are used to indicate a number of things that can be counted. If a carton says it contains 12 eggs, that number doesn't depend on a unit of measurement—12 eggs is 12 eggs (until you eat some for breakfast). A box of crayons is labeled with a large "96" because it contains 96 crayons—at least until some of them get broken, and then you might have 90 crayons plus 12 half crayons . . .

Numbers in the Real World

The world is also filled with things that aren't labeled with a numeral. And that is where **you** come in—you are the one who brings a number to life. The number representing a group of objects only has meaning if there's somebody looking at the objects, counting them, or wondering, "How many are there?" If you look at a flower, you might notice how beautiful it is, and you might also notice that it has, say, 5 petals. If you see a flock of geese overhead, you might admire the V formation they're flying in, and you may also count that there are 11 of them—or maybe you'll estimate that there are about 50, or 200 . . . or just too many to count. Everywhere you look there are things that could be counted—some easily, some with difficulty, and some only in theory. The world is full of numbers—1, 2, 3, a million, a quintillion—what fun!

0

Zero is a very strange number. It means "none" or "nothing." It's the number of cats living on the Moon, the number of fish who have climbed Mount Everest, and the number of dinosaurs roaming around New York City!

But 0 is not only a number that means the quantity of nothing. It also plays a central role in the place value–based number system we use today. For example, we write 605 to mean 6 hundreds, 0 tens, and 5 ones. The numbers 605 and 65 are definitely not the same, so the 0 is extremely important!

SAY IT! WRITE IT!

English: zero
Spanish: cero
Mandarin: líng
Tagalog: wala
Arabic: ṣifr
German: null

The number 0 was invented several thousand years after the natural numbers 1, 2, 3, etc. The idea of "none" being a number took a long time to catch on. Neither the ancient Babylonians, Egyptians, Greeks, nor Romans had a generally recognized symbol for 0. The ancient Mayans did—it looked like the image on the right.

But the way we use 0 today is thought to have developed in India around 700 CE. It was probably first written as a dot, as in this stone inscription of the number "605" written in Khmer numerals from 683 CE:

The first known use of a small circle to represent zero was in 876 CE in India. But it took several hundred more years for the 0 that we know and love to be used all over the world. Now we have a bunch of words that mean 0: *nada*, *zilch*, *zip*, *diddly*, and *diddly-squat*!

SHOW ME 0!

0 cookies

Braille:

American Sign Language:

-100
-90
-80
-70
-60
-50
-40
-30
-20
-10
0

WILD ABOUT 0!

Zero
CITY LIMIT
POP 0   ELEV 0

There are small communities named Zero in Montana and Mississippi. There used to be a town called Zero in Iowa—but sadly, its population is now 0.

Absolute zero is the lowest possible temperature. It equals 0 degrees Kelvin, or −273.15 degrees Celsius, or −459.67 degrees Fahrenheit.

In tennis, a score of 0 is called *love*. In other sports, especially baseball, a score of 0 is called a *goose egg*, because the numeral 0 looks like an egg. And in cricket, a score of 0 is called a *duck* (originally a *duck's egg*).

Zero Mostel was an American actor, comedian, and singer famous for his role in the Broadway musical *Fiddler on the Roof*.

In soccer, *nil* means a team score of 0 goals. A game that ends in a 0–0 tie would be described as *nil–nil*.

DO THE MATH!

0 is **even**.

0 is neither **prime** nor **composite**.

Factors: Mathematicians disagree on this—some say that 0 has **no factors**, but others say that **all** numbers are factors of 0!

0 is the *additive identity*, which means that adding 0 to a number does not change the number's value (think 2 + 0 = 2).

Tens	Ones
0	0

The number 1 is the foundation of counting; when we count 1, 2, 3 . . . we are adding 1 to each number to get the next number. Every counting number is built by adding 1 to itself over and over, like this:

$$1 = 1$$
$$2 = 1 + 1$$
$$3 = 1 + 1 + 1$$
$$4 = 1 + 1 + 1 + 1$$
$$5 = 1 + 1 + 1 + 1 + 1$$

SAY IT! WRITE IT!

English: one
Spanish: uno
Mandarin: yī
Swahili: moja

Roman: I
Babylonian: 𒁹
Ancient Greek: α

The number 1 is also special because when you multiply any number by 1, the product is that number. For example, $7 \times 1 = 7$. It's the only number that works this way. This is also true for division: When you divide any number by 1, the end result (the *quotient*) is the original number. So $7 \div 1 = 7$, and so on!

You can see the number 1 everywhere in the world. There are 1 sun and 1 moon in our sky, and there's only 1 planet Earth. And in all the world, there's only 1 you!

DO THE MATH!

1 is **odd**.

1 is neither prime nor composite—it's called a **unit**, and it's a very special number!

Tens	Ones
0	1

Factors: 1

1 is a square number, because $1 \times 1 = 1$. That means you can make a square with 1 dot; it'll have 1 row of dots, with 1 dot in each row.

1 is also a triangular number, since you can make a small triangle with 1 dot!

SHOW ME 1!

Braille:

1 whale

$1 \times 1 = 1$

100
90
80
70
60
50
40
30
20
10
1
0

WILD ABOUT 1!

Earth is the only planet in the solar system with exactly 1 moon. There are also some dwarf planets (including three named Eris, Makemake, and Gonggong) that have just 1 moon.

The prefix *uni-* means "1." It is used in words like *unicycle*, *unicorn*, *unique*, and *universe*.

We chant "**We're Number One!**" to say our favorite sports team is the best!

In a deck of cards, the ace can have a value of 1 or a value of 11—it's a tricky card!

The word "one" appears in many expressions in English. For example: *one-horse town*, *one-way street*, *one-way ticket*, and *one-track mind* (like someone who thinks about numbers all the time!).

American Sign Language:

1 H

Hydrogen is the chemical element with atomic number 1. An atom of hydrogen has 1 proton—that's why its atomic number is 1. It also has 1 electron and (usually) 0 neutrons. Hydrogen is the simplest element and by far the most abundant in the universe. All the stars out there, including our Sun, are made primarily of hydrogen. But on Earth, most hydrogen is combined with oxygen to make a rather important liquid called water!

2

So many things come in twos, starting with an average human body: 2 eyes and 2 ears; 2 hands and 2 feet; 2 arms and 2 legs. And the world is full of twos: peanut butter and jelly; salt and pepper; up and down; day and night; Dorothy and Toto; you and me . . . What examples can you think of? Groups of 2 are so important that we have many words for them, including *pair*, *couple*, *twosome*, *duo*, *brace*, *dyad*, *doublet*, and *twain*. And if 2 people play music, sing, or dance together, it's called a *duet*.

Look around and you'll see 2 everywhere. Sports cars that don't have a back seat are called *two-seaters*, and mopeds have two-stroke engines. Or maybe you would prefer a bicycle built for 2—you could ride it to the beach and go swimming in your two-piece bathing suit. After the beach, you could go dance the two-step. And if someone says you have two left feet, it means you aren't good at dancing—but don't believe it!

SAY IT! WRITE IT!

English: two
Spanish: dos
Tagalog: dalawa
Vietnamese: hai

Roman: II
Chinese: 二
Mayan: ••

DO THE MATH!

2 is **even**. $2 \div 2 = 1$

2 is **prime**.
Factors: 1 and 2

Tens	Ones
0	2

Numbers divisible by 2 are called *even* numbers.

Numbers **not** divisible by 2 are called *odd* numbers.

2 is the only even prime number!

SHOW ME 2!

1 + 1 = 2

2 is prime!

2 mice

WILD ABOUT 2!

The planet Mars and the dwarf planet Haumea each have 2 moons. We Earth dwellers have to be satisfied with only 1!

Two bits is an old-fashioned term for 25 cents. What is the value of one bit?

In card games, a card with a 2 on it is often called a *deuce*.

They say two heads are better than one . . . Do you agree?

Braille:

American Sign Language:

2 He

Helium is the chemical element with atomic number 2. An atom of helium has 2 protons, 2 electrons, and (usually) 2 neutrons. Helium is the secondmost abundant element in the universe. It is rare on Earth, but we use it to inflate balloons—and if you breathe it in and then talk, you sound like a mouse!

The number 3 is considered significant—even magical—in many cultures. For example, if you rub a magic lamp and a genie comes out, guess how many wishes you get? There's something about a group of 3 things that feels complete; some people call this the Rule of Three. Here are a few examples where a list of 3 things just sounds good: tic, tac, toe . . . reduce, reuse, recycle . . . lights, camera, action!

The number 3 is a central element of many folktales, myths, and other stories, and often appears in their titles, as in "The *Three* Little Pigs" or "Goldilocks and the *Three* Bears." And there are many *trios* (groups of three) in books, stories, and movies, like Harry, Ron, and Hermione.

You can also find the number 3 in many religions. In Christianity, the Holy Trinity is the doctrine of God existing as 3 entities—the Father, Son, and Holy Spirit. In Islam, there are 3 types of Sunnah: the sayings of the prophet Muhammad (Sunnah Qawliyyah, or Hadith), the actions of the prophet (Sunnah Al Filiyya), and the practices that the prophet approved (Sunnah Taqririyyah). In Judaism, the Three Patriarchs (Abraham, Isaac, and Jacob) are important ancestors of the Israelites. In Hinduism, the Trimurti is a trinity of male deities: Brahma, Vishnu, and Shiva; the Tridevi is a trinity of female deities: Saraswati, Lakshmi, and Parvati.

DO THE MATH!

3 is **odd**.

3 is **prime**.

Factors: 1 and 3

Tens	Ones
0	3

A whole number is divisible by 3 if the sum of its digits is divisible by 3. For example, 147 is divisible by 3 because $1 + 4 + 7 = 12$, which is divisible by 3.

3 and 5 are twin primes.

3 is a triangular number!

SHOW ME 3!

$2 + 1 = 3$

3 is prime!

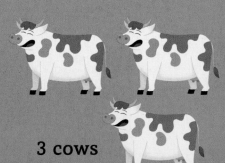

3 COWS

WILD ABOUT 3!

The number 3 comes up in many sports: In basketball, if you make a shot from beyond a certain distance, it's worth 3 points. In American and Canadian football, a field goal is worth 3 points. In soccer and hockey, if you score 3 goals in one game, it's called a *hat trick*. And in baseball, 3 strikes means you're out!

The prefix *tri-* means "3." It is used in words like *tricycle*, *triceratops*, *triple*, and *triathlon*.

Many objects, both natural and human-made, have threefold rotational symmetry, which looks like this:

A flat shape with straight sides is called a *polygon*, and a polygon with 3 sides is called, of course, a *triangle*! (But the word *triangle* actually means "3 angles," which is another way to look at it . . .) Here are some important types of triangles:

In card games, a card with a 3 on it is often called a *trey*.

 EQUILATERAL TRIANGLE

ISOSCELES TRIANGLE

 RIGHT TRIANGLE

Braille:

American Sign Language:

3
Li

Lithium is the chemical element with atomic number 3. An atom of lithium has 3 protons, 3 electrons, and (usually) 3 or 4 neutrons. Lithium has many uses, including in heat-resistant glass and ceramics; rechargeable batteries; and alloys with aluminum, copper, and other metals.

You may have noticed that lots of things come in fours. Most animals have 4 legs, and cars typically have 4 wheels. The ancient Greeks believed that everything was composed of 4 basic elements: fire, water, earth, and air. There are 4 cups in 1 quart, 4 quarts in 1 gallon, and 4 quarters in 1 dollar. Scientists tell us that there are 4 basic states of matter: solid, liquid, gas, and plasma. There are 4 seasons (spring, summer, fall, and winter), 4 cardinal/compass directions (north, east, south, and west), and even 4 members of the Beatles (John, Paul, George, and Ringo).

Some very important events happen once every 4 years, including the Olympic Games, the soccer World Cup, and the U.S. presidential election. And leap years follow the same pattern, like 2016, 2020, and 2024. So, if you're born on February 29, you have a birthday only once every 4 years!

A solid figure with flat faces is called a *polyhedron*; a polyhedron with 4 faces is called a *tetrahedron*.

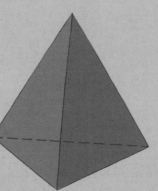

DO THE MATH!

4 is **even**. $4 \div 2 = 2$

4 is **composite**.

	Tens	Ones
Factors: 1, 2, and 4	0	4

Prime Factorization: 2×2

4 is a square number, because you can make a square with 2 rows of 2 dots. You can write this as $2 + 2 = 4$, or $2 \times 2 = 4$. They mean the same thing!

SHOW ME 4!

$3 + 1 = 4$

$2 \times 2 = 4$

$2 + 2 = 4$

4 cats

100
90
80
70
60
50
40
30
20
10
0

WILD ABOUT 4!

Four Corners is the spot where 4 U.S. states meet.

UTAH | COLORADO
ARIZONA | NEW MEXICO

The number 4 is important in baseball and softball. There are 4 bases on the field, 4 balls is a walk, and a grand slam scores 4 runs!

A shape made by joining 4 congruent squares along their edges is called a *tetromino*. (You may recognize them from the game *Tetris*.) There are five "free" tetrominoes:

Many musical instruments have 4 strings, including the violin, the double bass, and the ukulele. And a musical group with 4 members is called a *quartet*.

A polygon with 4 sides is called a *quadrilateral*—or sometimes, a *quadrangle*! Here are some types of quadrilaterals:

SQUARE

RECTANGLE

RHOMBUS

TRAPEZOID

PARALLELOGRAM

Braille:

American Sign Language:

4
Be

Beryllium is the chemical element with atomic number 4. It is alloyed with copper, nickel, and other elements to make metals that have many uses, including in spacecraft and communication satellites.

Look at your hand: How many fingers do you have? 5! Look at your foot: How many toes? 5! And when two people raise their hands and slap each other's palm, it's called a *high five*! Now think about how many senses the average human has. That's right, 5: sight, hearing, smell, taste, and touch. (These are the "classical" senses; scientists now say we have more than that.)

You'll also see the number 5 in many religions. The Five Pillars of Sunni Islam are practices of fundamental importance to Sunni Muslims all over the world. The Five Pillars are *Shahada* (Declaration of Faith), *Salah* (Prayer), *Zakat* (Almsgiving), *Sawm* (Fasting), and *Hajj* (Pilgrimage). In Hinduism, the god Shiva has 5 faces, and the 5 basic elements are earth, fire, water, air, and space. In Judaism, the Torah contains 5 books (Genesis, Exodus, Leviticus, Numbers, and Deuteronomy). And in Sikhism, there are 5 sacred symbols: kesh, kangha, kara, kachera, and kirpan.

The number 5 is important in geometry! A polygon with 5 sides is called a *pentagon*.

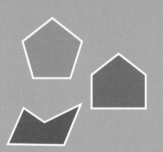

DO THE MATH!

5 is **odd**.

5 is **prime**.

Factors: 1 and 5

Tens	Ones
0	5

3 and 5 are twin primes, and so are 5 and 7.

A whole number is divisible by 5 if the digit in the ones place is 0 or 5. For example, 730 is divisible by 5 because its ones digit is 0.

SHOW ME 5!

4 + 1 = 5

3 + 2 = 5

5 is prime!

WILD ABOUT 5!

Check out the number 5 in sports! The symbol of the Olympic Games is a set of 5 interlocking rings. In rugby, a try is worth 5 points. And in basketball, each team has 5 players on the court at a time.

A musical group with 5 members is called a *quintet*.

There are 5 Great Lakes in North America: Superior, Michigan, Huron, Erie, and Ontario. And New York City is divided into 5 boroughs: the Bronx, Brooklyn, Manhattan, Queens, and Staten Island.

Most starfish have 5 . . . well, what are they? Arms? Legs? Appendages?

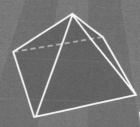

A polyhedron with 5 faces is called a *pentahedron*.

Braille:

American Sign Language:

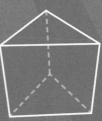

5 B

Boron is the chemical element with atomic number 5. Boron and its compounds have a great number of uses, including in magnets, semiconductors, glassmaking, cleaning products, antiseptics, and fire retardants.

Let's get acquainted with 6. Many flowers have 6 petals; snowflakes have 6 sides or points; and quartz crystals are shaped like hexagons (shapes with 6 sides). Insects are called *hexapods* because they have 6 legs.

When you go to the grocery store and buy a half dozen eggs, how many do you get? That's right, 6 eggs! That's because 6 is half of 12. For the same reason, 6 months is a half year, and 6 inches is a half foot. A standard guitar has 6 strings. And a group of 6 musicians is called a *sextet*. If the members of a sextet are all playing guitars, how many strings are there in all?

The ancient Greeks called 6 a *perfect number* because it equals the sum of its factors: $1 + 2 + 3 = 6$. (The next perfect number is 28.)

The *I Ching* is an ancient Chinese book used for fortune-telling. An important part of the *I Ching* is a series of 64 hexagrams. Each hexagram contains 6 lines, which are either solid lines (yang) or broken lines (yin). The first three hexagrams are shown below.

DO THE MATH!

6 is **even**. $6 \div 2 = 3$

6 is **composite**.

Factors:
1, 2, 3, and 6

Tens	Ones
0	6

Prime Factorization: 2×3

6 is a triangular number: $1 + 2 + 3 = 6$

6 is a centered pentagonal number:

SHOW ME 6!

$5 + 1 = 6$

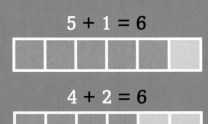

$4 + 2 = 6$

$3 + 3 = 6$

$2 \times 3 = 6$

$1 + 2 + 3 = 6$

6•

WILD ABOUT 6!

In a game of ice hockey, each team usually has 6 players on the ice.

Here are three hexagons; the first one is a *regular* hexagon (which means it has 6 equal sides).

A common piece of hardware is a 6-sided hex nut, which goes on a hex bolt.

Many natural and human-made objects have sixfold rotational symmetry, which looks like this:

The wax cells in a beehive are shaped like hexagons.

A 6-pointed star is called a *hexagram*. Notice that it can also be seen as two interlocking equilateral triangles. The hexagram has been used as a symbol in many religions.

Braille:

American Sign Language:

6

C

Carbon is the chemical element with atomic number 6. We have known of it since ancient times in the form of charcoal and soot—but diamonds are made of carbon, too. Carbon is an essential element in all known forms of life, and it's the secondmost abundant element in the human body.

7

Meet lucky number 7! Yes, 7 is considered a lucky number in many cultures. And it is much loved—in fact, a recent survey concluded that 7 is the most popular "favorite number."

The ancient city of Rome (now the capital of Italy) is called the "City of Seven Hills" because it was originally built on 7 hills. However, there are dozens of cities around the world that make the same claim!

The number 7 is significant in many religions. In Christianity, there are Seven Virtues: chastity, temperance, charity, diligence, kindness, patience, and humility. In Reform Judaism, the major holiday of Passover is traditionally celebrated for 7 days. Islamic pilgrims who visit Mecca walk 7 times around the Kaaba, and in Hinduism, the Saptarishi are the Seven Sages of ancient India. And in Japanese mythology, the Seven Lucky Gods are Ebisu, Daikokuten, Bishamonten, Hotei, Jurōjin, Benzaiten, and Fukurokuju—lucky number 7 again!

A polygon with 7 sides is called a *heptagon*.

SAY IT! WRITE IT!

English: seven
Spanish: siete
Vietnamese: bảy
Italian: sette

Roman: VII
Cherokee: ᏕᎭᎵᏆᎩ
Egyptian: |||| |||

DO THE MATH!

7 is **odd**.

7 is **prime**.

Factors: 1 and 7

Tens	Ones
0	7

7 is the difference of two square numbers: $16 - 9 = 7$.

5 and 7 are twin primes.

7 is a centered hexagonal number:

SHOW ME 7!

$6 + 1 = 7$

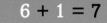

$5 + 2 = 7$

$4 + 3 = 7$

$2 + 3 + 2 = 7$

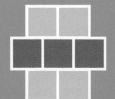

7 is prime!

7

WILD ABOUT 7!

In music, the major scale has 7 distinct notes: do, re, mi, fa, sol, la, and ti.

We generally consider there to be 7 colors in a rainbow: red, orange, yellow, green, blue, indigo, and violet.

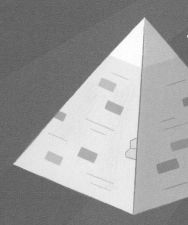

The Seven Wonders of the World in ancient times were the Great Pyramid of Giza, the Colossus of Rhodes, the Lighthouse of Alexandria, the Mausoleum at Halicarnassus, the Temple of Artemis, the Statue of Zeus at Olympia, and the Hanging Gardens of Babylon.

And of course, there are 7 days in a week!

Braille:

American Sign Language:

7 N

Nitrogen is the chemical element with atomic number 7. An atom of nitrogen has 7 protons, 7 electrons, and (usually) 7 neutrons. Nitrogen is a gas that makes up about 78 percent of Earth's atmosphere, and it's the fourthmost abundant element in the human body. Nitrogen is vital to life on Earth because it is a component of all proteins.

The number 8 was the star at the 2008 Olympic Games in Beijing, China! The opening ceremony began at 8:00 p.m. on 8/8/08. That's because 8 is considered a lucky number in Chinese culture.

Everywhere you look, 8 shows up. There are 8 fluid ounces in 1 cup, 8 pints in 1 gallon, and 8 furlongs in 1 mile (a furlong is 220 yards). You may have played a fun card game called Crazy Eights or the popular billiards (pool) game called Eight Ball. A group of 8 musicians is called an *octet*. A V-8 engine is a type of car engine with 8 cylinders arranged in a V shape. And the U.S. dollar used to be divided into 8 parts called *bits*, so 1 bit was worth 12.5 cents—isn't that strange?

The number 8 is important in many religions. In Buddhism, the Noble Eightfold Path is a series of 8 practices that were recommended by the Buddha. In Hinduism, the goddess Lakshmi traditionally appears in 8 different forms. In Judaism, the important winter holiday Hanukkah is celebrated for 8 days. In Christianity, the 8 (or sometimes 9) Beatitudes are sayings attributed to Jesus. And Islamic tradition describes *Jannah*, or Heaven, as having 8 doors or gates.

Finally, did you know there are 8 planets in our solar system? There used to be 9, but Pluto is now considered a dwarf planet!

SAY IT! WRITE IT!

English: eight
Spanish: ocho
Japanese: hachi
Urdu: aath

Roman: VIII
Chinese: 八
Aztec: ⋮

DO THE MATH!

8 is **even**. $8 \div 2 = 4$

8 is **composite**.

Factors:
1, 2, 4, and 8

Tens	Ones
0	8

Prime Factorization: $2 \times 2 \times 2$

8 is a cube number because $2 \times 2 \times 2 = 8$.

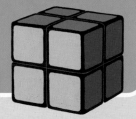

SHOW ME 8!

$7 + 1 = 8$

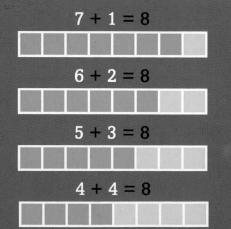

$6 + 2 = 8$

$5 + 3 = 8$

$4 + 4 = 8$

$2 \times 4 = 8$

$2 \times 2 \times 2 = 8$

WILD ABOUT 8!

Spiders (and other arachnids, like scorpions and ticks) have 8 legs. And of course, an octopus has 8 arms!

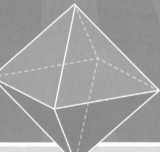

A "figure eight" describes anything in the shape of the numeral 8. Here's a figure eight knot:

Many natural and human-made objects have eightfold rotational symmetry, which looks like this:

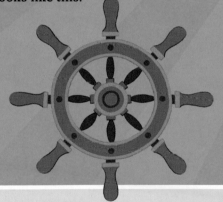

A polygon with 8 sides is called an *octagon*. The first octagon shown here is a *regular octagon*, which is the shape of a stop sign.

A polyhedron with 8 faces is called an *octahedron*.

Braille:

American Sign Language:

8
O

Oxygen is the chemical element with atomic number 8. Oxygen is a colorless, odorless gas. It's the most abundant element on Earth and the thirdmost abundant element in the universe. All plants and animals (including humans) need oxygen to live; we get it by breathing air, which is approximately 21 percent oxygen. Oxygen combines easily with other elements, forming many important compounds; most notably, it combines with hydrogen to make water.

You could say 9 is fine! The number 9 is used in many sayings. You may have heard that cats have 9 lives. To be "on cloud nine" means to be extremely happy. The "whole nine yards" means "everything" or "the entire amount." "Dressed to the nines" means to be all dressed up. And they say that "a stitch in time saves nine"!

In Greek mythology, the 9 Muses are goddesses who inspire artists and writers. In Norse mythology, the universe is divided into 9 worlds or realms. And in Christianity, there are said to be 9 choirs of angels.

More about 9: There are 9 justices on the Supreme Court of the United States (and the same in Canada). The 9th month of the year, September, has 9 letters in its name. And there's a town in Arkansas called Number Nine!

SAY IT! WRITE IT!

English: nine
Spanish: nueve
Mandarin: jiǔ
Tagalog: siyam

Roman: IX
Ancient Greek: θ
Mayan:

DO THE MATH!

9 is **odd**.

9 is **composite**.

Tens	Ones
0	9

Factors: 1, 3, and 9

Prime Factorization: 3×3

9 is a square number because $3 \times 3 = 9$.

A number is divisible by 9 if the sum of its digits is divisible by 9. For example, 4,617 is divisible by 9 because $4 + 6 + 1 + 7 = 18$, and 18 is divisible by 9.

A polygon with 9 sides is called a *nonagon*.

$8 + 1 = 9$

$7 + 2 = 9$

$6 + 3 = 9$

$5 + 4 = 9$

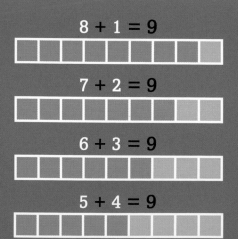

SHOW ME 9!

$6 + 3 = 9$

$3 \times 3 = 9$

WILD ABOUT 9!

There are 9 innings in a baseball game, and each team has 9 players.

In the Bahá'í faith, the number 9 symbolizes completeness, and a common symbol of the religion is a 9-pointed star.

Here's a picture of 9 cubes. But look closely: This arrangement is impossible!

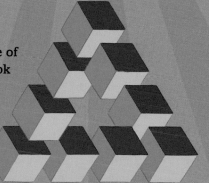

The famous composer Ludwig van Beethoven wrote 9 symphonies.

Braille:

American Sign Language:

9

F

Fluorine is the chemical element with atomic number 9. Fluorine is a pale yellow, highly reactive gas. Compounds of fluorine (such as sodium fluoride) are commonly added to drinking water and toothpaste to help prevent dental cavities. Other compounds of fluorine are used in high-temperature plastics such as Teflon.

10

All over the world, children learn to count to 10. We don't count to 9 or 11—it's always 10. The number 10 is the base of the decimal number system that we use today, probably because we have a total of 10 fingers on our two hands. We write numbers using ones, tens, hundreds, thousands, and so on—what we call *powers of 10*, because 10 × 10 = 100, 10 × 10 × 10 = 1,000, etc. For example, the number 3,456 means 3 thousands, 4 hundreds, 5 tens, and 6 ones.

In the United States, we use 10 in our money system, too—10 pennies equals 1 dime, and 10 dimes equals 1 dollar. Outside of the United States, most countries use the *metric system* of measurement, which is based on powers of 10. The basic units are the *meter* (length), the *gram* (mass or weight), and the *liter* (capacity). For example, 10 millimeters = 1 centimeter, 100 centimeters = 1 meter, and 1,000 meters = 1 kilometer.

There are 10 years in a decade, 10 decades in a century, and 10 centuries in a millennium. The first 10 amendments to the U.S. Constitution are called the Bill of Rights. In Judaism and Christianity, the Ten Commandments are a set of guiding principles given to Moses by God.

SAY IT! WRITE IT!

English: ten

Spanish: diez

Portuguese: dez

Hebrew:
  asara (masculine),
  eser (feminine)

Roman: X

Babylonian: ⟨

Egyptian: ∩

DO THE MATH!

10 is **even**. $10 \div 2 = 5$

10 is **composite**.

Factors:
1, 2, 5, and 10

Tens	Ones
1	0

Prime Factorization: 2×5

10 is a triangular number because $1 + 2 + 3 + 4 = 10$.

A number is divisible by 10 if its ones digit is 0. For example, 4,590 is divisible by 10.

SHOW ME 10!

$9 + 1 = 10$

$8 + 2 = 10$

$7 + 3 = 10$

$6 + 4 = 10$

$2 \times 5 = 10$

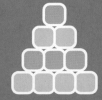

$1 + 2 + 3 + 4 = 10$

WILD ABOUT 10!

Did you know that cowboy hats are often called *10-gallon hats*? Do you think a cowboy hat could hold 10 gallons of water?

Crabs, lobsters, and shrimp are called *decapods* because they have 10 legs.

In athletics, the *decathlon* is a series of 10 track-and-field events contested in a two-day period. In basketball, the official height of the basket (or hoop) is 10 feet above the ground. And in bowling, 10 pins are arranged in the shape of a triangle, and you roll the ball and try to knock them all down!

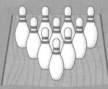

10 is a *tetrahedral* number because 1 + 3 + 6 = 10. You can make a tetrahedron by stacking triangular layers of 1, 3, and 6 spheres.

The term *sawbuck* is a slang word for a $10 bill. That's because a "sawbuck" or "sawhorse" resembles the Roman numeral symbol for 10: X.

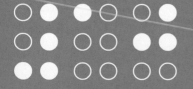

A polygon with 10 sides is called a *decagon*.

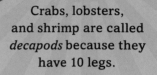

Braille:

American Sign Language:

Neon is the chemical element with atomic number 10. Neon is a *noble gas*, which means it does not usually combine with other elements. Neon is believed to be the fifthmost abundant element in the universe, but it is rare on Earth. Its main use is in brightly lit advertising signs, which are usually called—not surprisingly—*neon signs*.

You can write 11 backward or upside down, and it's still 11. The base of the Statue of Liberty is an 11-pointed star. In soccer, American football, cricket, and field hockey, each team has 11 players on the field. And the recipe for Colonel Sanders's Kentucky Fried Chicken is supposed to include a blend of "11 herbs and spices."

SHOW ME 11!

$5 + 5 + 1 = 11$

11 **is prime!**

DO THE MATH!

11 is **odd**.

11 is **prime**.

Factors:
1 and 11

Tens	Ones
1	1

Decompositions:
10 + 1; 9 + 2; 8 + 3; 7 + 4; and 6 + 5

11 and 13 are twin primes.

WILD ABOUT 11!

Apollo 11 was the first space mission to land human beings on the Moon.

An 11-sided polygon is called a *hendecagon* or an *undecagon*. The Susan B. Anthony dollar coin featured a hendecagon.

11
Na

Sodium is the chemical element with atomic number 11. It forms many important compounds, most notably sodium chloride, which we know as salt. Sodium is abundant on Earth, particularly in the form of salt in the ocean, and is an essential element for human health.

100
90
80
70
60
50
40
30
20
11 • 10
0

Can you see all 12 constellations in the zodiac? The *zodiac* is a belt-shaped region of the night sky. It is divided into 12 equal sections or *signs*, each named for a constellation. The practice of astrology is largely based on this system. The Chinese zodiac assigns animal names to years in a pattern that repeats every 12 years.

The number 12 is found in Greek mythology, where the 12 Olympians are gods who live on Mount Olympus. In the Hebrew Bible, Jacob has 12 sons, who are the progenitors of the Twelve Tribes of Israel. In the Christian tradition, Jesus has 12 apostles, and 12 days of Christmas are celebrated.

DO THE MATH!

12 is **even**. $12 \div 2 = 6$

12 is **composite**.

Factors:
1, 2, 3, 4, 6, and 12

Tens	Ones
1	2

$12 = 2 \times 6 = 3 \times 4$

Prime Factorization:
$2 \times 2 \times 3$

Decompositions:
$11 + 1$; $10 + 2$; $9 + 3$; $8 + 4$; $7 + 5$; and $6 + 6$

SHOW ME 12!

$2 \times 2 \times 3 = 12$

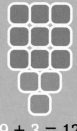

$9 + 3 = 12$

WILD ABOUT 12!

In the United States, juries often consist of 12 people who make decisions in court trials.

A year has 12 months. And each day has two 12-hour periods, which is why analog clocks are numbered from 1 to 12.

12
Mg

Magnesium has the atomic number 12. Magnesium alloys have many uses, including in car engines, cell phones, and computers.

The "12-bar blues" is a style of music that's divided into short sections called *bars*, and the overall pattern of the music repeats after 12 bars.

100
90
80
70
60
50
40
30
20
● 12
10
0

13

In many countries, 13 is considered an unlucky number. In fact, the word *triskaidekaphobia* means "fear of the number 13." But in Italy, 13 is seen as a lucky number!

Even though some people consider it unlucky, 13 is still everywhere. In a standard deck of playing cards, there are 13 hearts, 13 diamonds, 13 spades, and 13 clubs. And at the grocery store, a *baker's dozen* means 13—if you buy a dozen doughnuts from some bakers, you get 1 extra! The Hawaiian alphabet has 13 letters: A, E, I, O, U, H, K, L, M, N, P, W, and ' (the 'okina).

SAY IT! WRITE IT!

English: thirteen
Spanish: trece
Mandarin: shísān
Russian: trinadtsat'
___
Roman: XIII
Ancient Greek: ιγ
Egyptian: ∩||||

SHOW ME 13!

13 is prime!

$$9 + 4 = 13$$

DO THE MATH!

13 is **odd**.
13 is **prime**.
Factors:
1 and 13

Tens	Ones
1	3

Decompositions:
12 + 1; 11 + 2; 10 + 3; 9 + 4; 8 + 5; and 7 + 6
13 is the sum of two square numbers: 9 + 4 = 13.
11 and 13 are twin primes.

WILD ABOUT 13!

The original 13 United States colonies are represented by the 13 stripes on the U.S. flag: 7 red stripes and 6 white stripes. And the Great Seal of the United States features 13 stars, 13 stripes, 13 arrows, 13 leaves, and 13 olives.

Some species of cicada spend most of their lives underground, only emerging to spend a few weeks aboveground in the spring of their 13th year.

13
Al

Aluminum is the chemical element with atomic number 13. Aluminum has a great number of uses, including in aluminum foil, soft-drink cans, kitchen utensils and cooking pots, window frames, aircraft, boats, and more.

13

SAY IT! WRITE IT!

English: fourteen

Spanish: catorce

Tagalog: labing-apat

Arabic: arba'a 'ashar

Roman: XIV

Chinese: 十四

Ge'ez: ፲፬

William Shakespeare is known best for his amazing plays, but his sonnets are famous, too. A *sonnet* is a classical type of poem that traditionally has 14 lines. And if you read through any of Shakespeare's plays, you may come across the old-fashioned word *fortnight*, which is a unit of time equal to 14 days (or 14 nights)—the same as 2 weeks.

And have you seen any of the 96 *fourteeners* in the United States? Fourteeners are mountain peaks with heights over 14,000 feet.

DO THE MATH!

14 is **even**. $14 \div 2 = 7$

14 is **composite**.

Factors: 1, 2, 7, and 14

Tens	Ones
1	4

Prime Factorization: 2×7

Decompositions: $13 + 1$; $12 + 2$; $11 + 3$; $10 + 4$; $9 + 5$; $8 + 6$; and $7 + 7$

14 is the sum of the first three squares: $1 + 4 + 9 = 14$.

SHOW ME 14!

$2 \times 7 = 14$

$1 + 4 + 9 = 14$

WILD ABOUT 14!

The planet Neptune has 14 known moons.

In the United Kingdom, 1 *stone* is a unit of weight equal to 14 pounds.

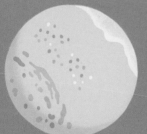

14 POUNDS

14 **Si**

Silicon is the chemical element with atomic number 14. Silicon and oxygen combine to make a variety of silicate minerals that humans have used for thousands of years in the forms of sand, clay, and rock. Silicon is an essential element in modern technology, such as smartphones and computers. Many people say we are living in the Silicon Age!

100

90

80

70

60

50

40

30

20

●14

10

0

If you've ever heard someone say "quarter past two," then you've definitely come into contact with the number 15! That's because there are 15 minutes in a quarter of an hour (since $4 \times 15 = 60$). We say "a quarter past" to mean 15 minutes after the hour, and "a quarter to" to mean 15 minutes before the hour.

The number 15 is also commonly found in sports. In American and Canadian football, games are divided into 15-minute quarters. And in tennis, if you win one point, your score is 15!

SAY IT! WRITE IT!

English: fifteen
Spanish: quince
French: quinze
Gujarati: pandar
_____
Roman: XV
Babylonian: 𒐕𒌋𒐏
Mayan: ≡

SHOW ME 15!

$3 \times 5 = 15$

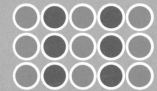

$9 + 6 = 15$

DO THE MATH!

15 is **odd**.

15 is **composite**.

Factors:
1, 3, 5, and 15

Tens	Ones
1	5

Prime Factorization: 3×5

Decompositions: 14 + 1; 13 + 2; 12 + 3; 11 + 4; 10 + 5; 9 + 6; and 8 + 7

15 is a triangular number: $1 + 2 + 3 + 4 + 5 = 15$.

WILD ABOUT 15!

15 is the number of billiard balls usually used in a game of pool (not counting the white cue ball), and they are numbered 1 through 15. At the start of the game, the 15 balls are arranged in a triangle.

15
P

Phosphorus is the chemical element with atomic number 15. It is essential to life, and its most important use is in agricultural fertilizers. Phosphorus is also found in safety matches, fireworks, cleaning agents, steel, and fine china.

A *quinceañera* means "15 years" in Spanish and is a Latin American celebration of a girl's 15th birthday.

SAY IT! WRITE IT!

English: sixteen
Spanish: dieciséis
Vietnamese: mười sáu
Punjabi: sōḷāṃ

Roman: XVI
Khmer: ១៦
Egyptian: ∩||||

If you've ever played chess, then you've seen the number 16. Each player in chess begins the game with 16 pieces. The number 16 is also important in measurements—there are 16 ounces in 1 pound, 16 fluid ounces in 1 pint, and 16 cups in 1 gallon. And if you take a look at a United States or world map, you'll see the number 16 again and again! In fact, there are towns named Sixteen in both Kentucky and Montana, and at least six creeks called Sixteen Mile Creek in North America. And many countries are divided into 16 parts, including Chile, Ghana, and Poland.

DO THE MATH!

16 is **even**. $16 \div 2 = 8$

16 is **composite**.

Factors: 1, 2, 4, 8, and 16

Tens	Ones
1	6

$16 = 2 \times 8 = 4 \times 4$

Prime Factorization: $2 \times 2 \times 2 \times 2$

Decompositions: 15 + 1; 14 + 2; 13 + 3; 12 + 4; 11 + 5; 10 + 6; 9 + 7; and 8 + 8

16 is a square number: $4 \times 4 = 16$.

16 is the 4th power of 2, because $2 \times 2 \times 2 \times 2 = 16$.

SHOW ME 16!

$4 \times 4 = 16$

$2 \times 2 \times 2 \times 2 = 16$

WILD ABOUT 16!

"Number 16" was the name of a female trapdoor spider observed by scientists in Western Australia. She lived for a record 43 years!

The Imperial Seal of Japan is a chrysanthemum flower with 16 petals in the front, plus another 16 petals behind those.

The maximum weight of a bowling ball is 16 pounds.

16
S

Sulfur has the atomic number 16. Pure sulfur has no smell, but many of its compounds have unpleasant odors—including the smells of skunks and rotten eggs. Sulfur has many uses, including in car batteries and fertilizers.

100
90
80
70
60
50
40
30
20
● 16
10
0

In a regular season for the NFL (National Football League), each team plays 17 games. A standard B-flat clarinet has 17 keys. And a day on Uranus is just 17 hours long.

A *koto* is a Japanese musical instrument that often has 17 strings. A *haiku* is a type of poem invented in Japan that traditionally has 17 syllables—usually in a 5, 7, 5 pattern.

SHOW ME 17!

16 + 1 = 17

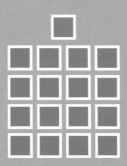

17 is prime!

DO THE MATH!

17 is **odd**.

17 is **prime**.

Factors:
1 and 17

Tens	Ones
1	7

Decompositions: 16 + 1; 15 + 2; 14 + 3; 13 + 4; 12 + 5; 11 + 6; 10 + 7; and 9 + 8

17 and 19 are twin primes.

WILD ABOUT 17!

The state flag of Ohio has 17 stars on it because Ohio was the 17th state to enter the Union.

The *stegosaurus* was a dinosaur with 17 bony plates on its back (or sometimes more)!

17
Cl

Chlorine is the chemical element with atomic number 17. It is used to make drinking water safe and to treat swimming pools. Chlorine also combines with sodium to produce something you probably eat every day: salt.

100
90
80
70
60
50
40
30
20
17●
10
0

SAY IT! WRITE IT!

English: eighteen
Spanish: dieciocho
Bengali: āṭhāra
Hawaiian: ʻumikūmāwalu

Roman: XVIII
Chinese: 十八
Arabic: ١٨

When you turn 18, you're considered an adult in many countries. In the United States, for example, the right to vote begins at age 18.

You'll also find the number 18 in various religious texts and cultures around the world. For example, the *Bhagavad Gita* is an ancient Hindu scripture that has 18 chapters. It is part of the epic *Mahābhārata*, which is divided into 18 books.

DO THE MATH!

18 is **even**. $18 \div 2 = 9$

18 is **composite**.

Factors: 1, 2, 3, 6, 9, and 18

Tens	Ones
1	8

$18 = 2 \times 9 = 3 \times 6$

Prime Factorization:
$2 \times 3 \times 3$

Decompositions: 17 + 1; 16 + 2; 15 + 3; 14 + 4; 13 + 5; 12 + 6; 11 + 7; 10 + 8; and 9 + 9

18 is twice a square number: $2 \times 9 = 18$.

SHOW ME 18!

$3 \times 6 = 18$

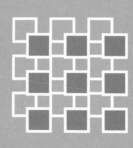

$2 \times 9 = 18$

WILD ABOUT 18!

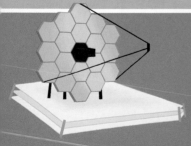

The James Webb Space Telescope uses an arrangement of 18 hexagonal mirrors made of gold-plated beryllium.

18

Ar

Argon is the chemical element with atomic number 18. It is used in light bulbs, arc welding, and medical lasers.

A golf course usually has 18 holes that are divided into two *nines*. A basketball hoop has a diameter of 18 inches. Volleyballs are made with 18 panels of leather, and the volleyball court is 18 meters long.

19

Look around and you just may find the number 19! The board game Go is played on a 19 by 19 grid of lines. In England, if you're *talking nineteen to the dozen*, it means you're talking very fast (perhaps using 19 words in the time it would usually take to say 12). The longest known palindrome word (written the same backward as forward) is a Finnish word with 19 letters: *saippuakivikauppias*. And the calendar used in the Bahá'í faith has 19 months, each with 19 days!

SAY IT! WRITE IT!

English: nineteen
Spanish: diecinueve
Haitian Creole: diz nèf
Serbo-Croatian: devetnaest

Roman: XIX
Mayan:
Devanagari: १९

SHOW ME 19!

19 **is** prime!

10 + 6 + 3 = 19

DO THE MATH!

19 is **odd**.

19 is **prime**.

Factors: 1 and 19

Tens	Ones
1	9

Decompositions:
18 + 1; 17 + 2; 16 + 3; 15 + 4; 14 + 5; 13 + 6; 12 + 7; 11 + 8; and 10 + 9

19 is the difference of two squares: 100 − 81 = 19.

17 and 19 are twin primes.

WILD ABOUT 19!

19 Fortuna is one of the largest asteroids in the asteroid belt. It was discovered in 1852 and named after the Roman goddess of good luck.

Since 19 is a centered hexagonal number, you will often see 19 things arranged in a hexagonal shape—for example, in sink and tub drains.

The state flag of Indiana has 19 stars on it because Indiana was the 19th state to enter the Union.

19
K

Potassium is the chemical element with atomic number 19. Because it's an essential element for living cells, potassium is an important nutrient for humans. It is a common ingredient in fertilizers and has many other uses, including in cleaning products, food additives, batteries, and glass.

100
90
80
70
60
50
40
30
20
10
0

19

20

SAY IT! WRITE IT!

English: twenty

Spanish: veinte

Persian (Farsi): bist

Lao: saao

Roman: XX

Hebrew: כ

Egyptian: ∩∩

The number 20 is found every-where. Ever heard of 20/20 vision? If you have it, you can read letters of a certain size from 20 feet away. When you were little, you probably grew 20 baby teeth—one painful tooth at a time! You may have played the guessing game called Twenty Questions. In old times, a *score* was another way to say 20. And if you call someone in Egypt, you'll use 20 as the calling code!

DO THE MATH!

20 is **even**. $20 \div 2 = 10$

20 is **composite**.

Tens	Ones
2	0

Factors: 1, 2, 4, 5, 10, and 20

$20 = 2 \times 10 = 4 \times 5$

Prime Factorization: $2 \times 2 \times 5$

Decompositions: $19 + 1$; $18 + 2$; $17 + 3$; $16 + 4$; $15 + 5$; $14 + 6$; $13 + 7$; $12 + 8$; $11 + 9$; and $10 + 10$

20 is called an *oblong number* because it's twice a triangular number: $10 + 10 = 20$.

20 is the sum of two squares: $16 + 4 = 20$.

SHOW ME 20!

$10 + 10 = 20$

$4 \times 5 = 20$

$2 \times 2 \times 5 = 20$

WILD ABOUT 20!

A dartboard is divided into 20 equal sections.

In the system of British money used until 1971, there were 20 shillings in 1 pound.

20 Ca

Calcium is the chemical element with atomic number 20. Calcium is the fifthmost abundant element in Earth's crust; its compounds appear as chalk, marble, and limestone. It's also an essential human nutrient, of particular importance for our muscles, bones, and teeth.

21

If you're opening this book between the years 2024 and 2100, then you're reading it in the 21st century! You may have also played the popular card game Twenty-One, featuring this fabulous number in its title. And did you know that there are 21 letters in the Italian alphabet?

SAY IT! WRITE IT!

English: twenty-one

Spanish: veintiuno

Mandarin: èr shí yī

Tagalog: dalawampu't isa

Roman: XXI

Ancient Greek: κα

Babylonian: 𒌋𒐖

SHOW ME 21!

$3 \times 7 = 21$

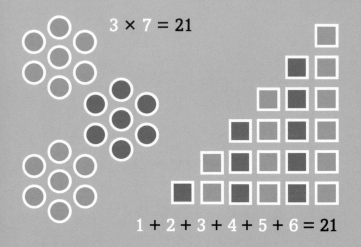

$1 + 2 + 3 + 4 + 5 + 6 = 21$

DO THE MATH!

21 is **odd**.

21 is **composite**.

Factors: 1, 3, 7, and 21

Tens	Ones
2	1

Prime Factorization: 3×7

21 is a triangular number because $21 = 1 + 2 + 3 + 4 + 5 + 6$.

WILD ABOUT 21!

In a game of badminton, at least 21 points are needed to win.

21
Sc

Scandium is the chemical element with atomic number 21. Alloys of scandium and aluminum are used to make baseball bats.

The flag of Kurdistan features a sun with 21 rays. The number 21 is a sacred symbol of rebirth in Kurdish culture.

(number line on left side)
100 — 90 — 80 — 70 — 60 — 50 — 40 — 30 — 21 • 20 — 10 — 0

SAY IT! WRITE IT!

English: twenty-two

Spanish: veintidós

Arabic: ithnan wa-'ishrun

Hindi: baees

Roman: XXII

Chinese: 二十二

Armenian: ԻԲ

A "catch-22" is a no-win situation; the term comes from the title of a famous novel. There are 22 letters in the Hebrew alphabet. In the game of cricket, the wickets are 22 yards apart. And with six straight cuts, you can slice a pancake into as many as 22 pieces!

SHOW ME 22!

DO THE MATH!

22 is **even**. 22 ÷ 2 = 11

22 is **composite**.

Factors: 1, 2, 11, and 22

Tens	Ones
2	2

Prime Factorization: 2 × 11

22 is the sum of a square number and a triangular number: 16 + 6 = 22.

$$16 + 6 = 22$$

$$2 \times 11 = 22$$

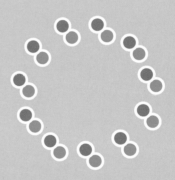

WILD ABOUT 22!

In a game of soccer, there are usually a total of 22 players on the field.

There are exactly 22 bones in a human skull!

22 Ti

Titanium is the chemical element with atomic number 22. Titanium is a strong, light metal with many uses, including in parts of boats, airplanes, and rockets.

Snooker is a type of billiards game that uses 22 balls.

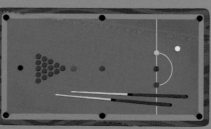

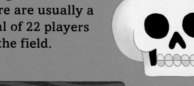

100 — 90 — 80 — 70 — 60 — 50 — 40 — 30 — ● 22 — 20 — 10 — 0

23

The number 23 seems pretty harmless...but the word *eikositriophobia* means "fear of the number 23." In the early 20th century, *23 skidoo* was a popular term meaning "to leave quickly." Before LeBron James changed his jersey number to 6 in 2021, he donned the number 23 for the Los Angeles Lakers. And a polygon with 23 sides is called an *icositrigon*!

SHOW ME 23!

$$5 \times 5 - 2 = 23$$

23 is prime!

DO THE MATH!

23 is **odd**.

23 is **prime**.

Factors: 1 and 23

Tens	Ones
2	3

23 is the smallest prime number without a twin prime.

WILD ABOUT 23!

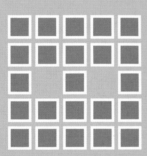

Most human body cells have 46 chromosomes that are arranged in 23 pairs. Chromosomes carry all the genes that determine who we are and what we look like.

Earth's axis is tilted about 23 degrees from the perpendicular, which is the main reason our weather varies with each season.

23.5°

NORTH POLE

EQUATOR

SOUTH POLE

23

V

Vanadium is the chemical element with atomic number 23. Vanadium is a soft, malleable metal mainly used in steel alloys. These alloys are used in cutting tools, jet engines, and automobiles, including in the original Ford Model T!

24

SAY IT! WRITE IT!

English: twenty-four
Spanish: veinticuatro
Korean: seumul net
French: vingt-quatre

Roman: XXIV
Thai: ๒๔
Egyptian: ∩∩IIII

To find the number 24 in your life, you'll only have to count the hours in a day; there are 24 hours each and every day, which is approximately how long it takes Earth to spin around one time. For the same reason, there are 24 time zones on our planet.

If you buy 2 dozen eggs, that's 24 eggs. A game of checkers starts with 24 checkers on the board; there are 24 letters in the Greek alphabet; pure gold is called 24-karat gold; and human beings have 12 pairs of ribs (for a total of 24)!

DO THE MATH!

24 is **even**. $24 \div 2 = 12$

24 is **composite**.

Factors: 1, 2, 3, 4, 6, 8, 12, and 24

Tens	Ones
2	4

$24 = 2 \times 12 = 3 \times 8 = 4 \times 6$

Prime Factorization:
$2 \times 2 \times 2 \times 3$

24 is the smallest number with 8 or more factors.

24 is the difference of two squares: $49 - 25 = 24$.

SHOW ME 24!

$16 + 4 + 4 = 24$

$2 \times 2 \times 2 \times 3 = 24$

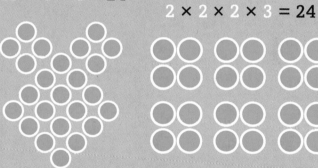

WILD ABOUT 24!

Have you heard the nursery rhyme about "four and twenty blackbirds baked in a pie"? It comes from a traditional English nursery rhyme called "Sing a Song of Sixpence."

A famous American racehorse named Four-and-Twenty won many California races in the 1960s.

24 **Cr**

Chromium is the chemical element with atomic number 24. It is an ingredient in stainless steel and other important alloys. For example, chromium plating is used to protect cars and bicycles.

100
90
80
70
60
50
40
30
•24
20
10
0

If you look around, you find 25 in the strangest places! Did you know that there are 25 counties named Franklin County in the United States?

To be elected to the U.S. House of Representatives, you must be at least 25 years old. In Islam, there are 25 prophets mentioned in the Koran. And the famous singer and song-writer Adele released an album called *25*, even though she was not 25 when she released it . . . she was 27!

SAY IT! WRITE IT!

English: twenty-five

Spanish: veinticinco

Russian: dvadtsat' pyat'

Japanese: ni-jū go

Roman: XXV

Ancient Greek: ΚΕ

Aztec:

SHOW ME 25!

$5 \times 5 = 25$

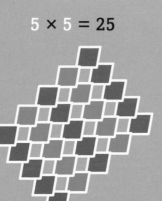

$15 + 10 = 25$

DO THE MATH!

25 is **odd**.

25 is **composite**.

Factors: 1, 5, and 25

Tens	Ones
2	5

Prime Factorization: 5×5

25 is a square number: $5 \times 5 = 25$.

25 is the sum of two squares: $16 + 9 = 25$.

WILD ABOUT 25!

A quarter has a value of 25 cents (and equals a quarter of a dollar).

25 **Mn**

Manganese is the chemical element with atomic number 25. It is found in small amounts in the human body.

A popular game in India is called pachisi, a name that comes from the Hindi word for 25, which is the largest score you can throw with the game's cowrie shells.

100
90
80
70
60
50
40
30
25
20
10
0

SAY IT! WRITE IT!

English: twenty-six
Spanish: veintiséis
Mandarin: èrshíliù
Italian: ventisei

Roman: XXVI
Babylonian: 𒌋𒌋𒐚
Cistercian: ⅂⌐

The number 26 is important in English because there are 26 letters in our alphabet. And they all appear in this sentence: "The quick brown fox jumps over the lazy dog." If you play cards, you might know that a standard deck has 26 red cards and 26 black cards. A marathon running race is just over 26 miles long, and if you train for 26 weeks, that's half of a year. And the longest common word in Italian is *precipitevolissimevolmente*, which has 26 letters and means "very, very, very quickly"!

DO THE MATH!

26 is **even**. $26 \div 2 = 13$

26 is **composite**.

Factors: 1, 2, 13, and 26

Tens	Ones
2	6

Prime Factorization: 2×13

26 is the sum of a square number and a triangular number: $16 + 10 = 26$.

SHOW ME 26!

$9 + 9 + 4 + 4 = 26$

$16 + 10 = 26$

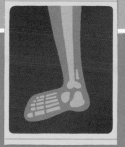

There are 26 bones in a human foot.

WILD ABOUT 26!

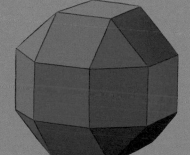

A *rhombicuboctahedron* is a solid figure with 26 faces. It has 8 triangular faces, 6 square faces, and 12 rectangular faces.

26
Fe

Iron is the chemical element with atomic number 26. Iron has been used for centuries to make tools for agriculture and hunting, and was even mentioned in Greek folklore and mythology. Archaeologists often speak of the "Iron Age" to describe a certain period in human history when the use of iron was of primary importance.

100
90
80
70
60
50
40
30
● 26
20
10
0

27

The number 27 shows up in space—the planet Uranus has 27 moons. Closer to home, did you know a human hand has 27 bones? Or that the width of a tennis court is 27 feet (for singles play)? There are lots of twenty-sevens in the Bible. In the Old Testament, Proverbs 27 has 27 verses, and the Book of Leviticus has 27 chapters; the New Testament has 27 books. The U.S. Constitution has 27 amendments (so far). And the Spanish alphabet has 27 letters—*muy bien*!

SAY IT! WRITE IT!

English: twenty-seven

Spanish: veintisiete

Tagalog: dalawampu't pito

Polish: dwadzieścia siedem

Roman: XXVII

Tamil: ௨௭

Ancient Greek: κζ

SHOW ME 27!

$3 \times 3 \times 3 = 27$

$3 \times 3 \times 3 = 27$

DO THE MATH!

27 is **odd**.

27 is **composite**.

Factors: 1, 3, 9, and 27

Tens	Ones
2	7

Prime Factorization: $3 \times 3 \times 3$

27 is a cube number because $3 \times 3 \times 3 = 27$.

WILD ABOUT 27!

The composer Wolfgang Amadeus Mozart wrote 27 concertos for piano and orchestra.

NGC 27 is a spiral galaxy located in the constellation Andromeda.

27
Co

Cobalt is the chemical element with atomic number 27. Cobalt has been used for centuries to give a blue color to glass and ceramics. It's also used in aircraft engines, batteries, and medical treatments. The name cobalt comes from the German *kobold*, a mythical goblin or sprite from German folklore.

28

SAY IT! WRITE IT!

English: twenty-eight

Spanish: veintiocho

Thai: yi sip paet

Hebrew: 'esrim ve shmone

Roman: XXVIII

Mayan: ⠒⠒

Chinese: 二十八

The number 28 has been around a long time—the ancient Greeks called 28 a *perfect number* because it's equal to the sum of its factors: $1 + 2 + 4 + 7 + 14 = 28$! And in the ancient Egyptian system for measuring length, there were 28 *digits* in 1 *royal cubit* (a digit was approximately the breadth of a human finger). February usually has 28 days (or exactly 4 weeks); the Arabic alphabet has 28 letters; and the English word *antidisestablishmentarianism* has 28 letters—try to spell that one!

DO THE MATH!

28 is **even**. $28 \div 2 = 14$

28 is **composite**.

Factors:
1, 2, 4, 7, 14, and 28

Tens	Ones
2	8

$28 = 2 \times 14 = 4 \times 7$

Prime Factorization: $2 \times 2 \times 7$

28 is a triangular number because $1 + 2 + 3 + 4 + 5 + 6 + 7 = 28$.

SHOW ME 28!

$2 \times 2 \times 7 = 28$

$1 + 2 + 3 + 4 + 5 + 6 + 7 = 28$

WILD ABOUT 28!

A set of dominoes usually has 28 domino tiles.

Gravity is 28 times as strong on the surface of the Sun as it is on Earth. You would feel very heavy (and hot!) on the surface of the Sun.

28
Ni

Nickel is the chemical element with atomic number 28. It is combined with other metals to make alloys that have many uses—including in the U.S. five-cent coin (also known as a nickel)!

100

90

80

70

60

50

40

30 — ●28

20

10

0

29

In the game of cribbage, 29 is the highest possible score for one hand; I bet they like cribbage in the city of Twentynine Palms, California. Where else can we find 29? In a leap year, February has 29 days. The Turkish, Finnish, Swedish, and Danish alphabets all have 29 letters. And the Atlanta Braves scored 29 runs in a baseball game against the Miami Marlins in 2020.

SHOW ME 29!

$$25 + 4 = 29$$

29 **is prime!**

DO THE MATH!

29 is **odd**.

29 is **prime**.

Factors: 1 and 29

Tens	Ones
2	9

29 is the sum of two squares: $25 + 4 = 29$.

29 and 31 are twin primes.

WILD ABOUT 29!

It takes Saturn about 29 years to orbit the Sun.

29 is a *Sophie Germain prime* because if you multiply it by 2, then add 1, you get another prime: $29 \times 2 + 1 = 59$. Sophie Germain was a French mathematician who lived from 1776 to 1831.

Sophie Germain

29
Cu

Copper is the chemical element with atomic number 29. Copper was probably the first metal used by humans; for thousands of years we've turned it into jewelry, sculptures, tools, bells, lamps, cookware, and coins. Its leading use today is in electrical wiring.

30

SAY IT! WRITE IT!

English: thirty

Spanish: treinta

Vietnamese: ba mươi

Portuguese: trinta

Roman: XXX

Ge'ez: ፴

Egyptian: ∩∩
∩

The number 30 is a *square pyramidal* number—if you have 30 tennis balls, you can build a square pyramid. It will have 4 levels, with a square number of tennis balls on each level: $16 + 9 + 4 + 1 = 30$.

There are 30 letters in the Bulgarian alphabet, and 30 is the international calling code for Greece. There are 30 songs on the Beatles' *White Album*. The minimum age for a U.S. senator is 30. A half hour is 30 minutes; half a minute is 30 seconds; and you've probably heard this rhyme: "Thirty days hath September, April, June and November."

DO THE MATH!

30 is **even**. $30 \div 2 = 15$

30 is **composite**.

Factors: 1, 2, 3, 5, 6, 10, 15, and 30

Tens	Ones
3	0

$30 = 2 \times 15 = 3 \times 10 = 5 \times 6$

Prime Factorization: $2 \times 3 \times 5$

30 is twice a triangular number: $2 \times 15 = 30$.

SHOW ME 30!

$15 + 15 = 30$

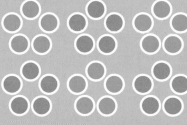

$2 \times 3 \times 5 = 30$

WILD ABOUT 30!

Adult cats usually have 30 teeth.

In a game of tennis, if you win two points, your score is 30!

30 Zn

Zinc is the chemical element with atomic number 30. Zinc is commonly used as a protective coating on iron or steel. It is also a component of metal alloys that have many uses, including in communication equipment, hardware, and musical instruments. Zinc is also an essential element in the human diet. Oysters have lots of zinc.

31

Did you know that Mexico has 31 states (not counting Mexico City)? And in French, "to put on one's thirty-one" means to get dressed up. In mathematics, a polygon with 31 sides is called a *triacontahenagon*. You'll find 31 on the calendar, too, because January, March, May, July, August, October, and December each have 31 days. And when California entered the Union in 1850, the U.S. flag had 31 stars—2 rows of 7, 2 rows of 6, and 1 row of 5!

SAY IT! WRITE IT!

English: thirty-one

Spanish: treinta y uno

Arabic: wahid wa-thalathun

Korean: seoreun hana

Roman: XXXI

Ancient Greek: λα

Chinese: 三十一

SHOW ME 31!

31 is prime!

$$21 + 10 = 31$$

DO THE MATH!

31 is **odd**.

31 is **prime**.

Factors: 1 and 31

Tens	Ones
3	1

29 and 31 are twin primes.

31 is the sum of two triangular numbers: 21 + 10 = 31.

WILD ABOUT 31!

Galaxy M31, the Andromeda Galaxy, is the nearest large galaxy to our own Milky Way.

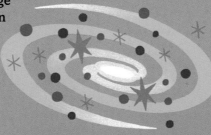

| 31 |
| Ga |

Gallium is the chemical element with atomic number 31. Gallium is a metal that is liquid above 85 degrees Fahrenheit, so it is sometimes used in high-temperature thermometers. But gallium is mainly used in the electronics industry to help make things like televisions and cell phones.

SPEED LIMIT 31

The city of Trenton, Tennessee, has streets with a speed limit of 31 miles per hour.

31

32

32

SAY IT! WRITE IT!

English: thirty-two

Spanish: treinta y dos

Tamil: muppatti iraṇṭu

Navajo: tádiin dóó ba'aan naaki

Roman: XXXII

Mayan: •• (with bar)

Khmer: ៣២

In sports, 32 comes up a lot! The National Football League currently has 32 teams, and so does the National Hockey League. And as of 2024, the soccer teams competing in the FIFA Men's and Women's World Cup come from 32 different nations.

The freezing point of water is 32 degrees Fahrenheit; an adult human typically has 32 teeth (including wisdom teeth, which are often removed); and in Hinduism, the elephant-headed god, Ganesha, is said to appear in 32 different forms.

DO THE MATH!

32 is **even**. $32 \div 2 = 16$

32 is **composite**.

Factors:
1, 2, 4, 8, 16, 32

Tens	Ones
3	2

$32 = 2 \times 16 = 4 \times 8$

Prime Factorization:
$2 \times 2 \times 2 \times 2 \times 2$

32 = 2 to the 5th power: $2 \times 2 \times 2 \times 2 \times 2$.

32 is twice a square number: $2 \times 16 = 32$.

SHOW ME 32!

$$2 \times 2 \times 2 \times 2 \times 2 = 32$$

$$16 + 16 = 32$$

WILD ABOUT 32!

A soccer ball is typically made by sewing together 32 panels (20 hexagons and 12 pentagons).

32
Ge

Germanium is the chemical element with atomic number 32. Germanium is a gray-white metalloid important in fiber optics and in the semiconductor (computer) industry, It is named for Germany—but you probably guessed that!

In the game of chess, there are a total of 32 pieces, and the chessboard has 32 black squares and 32 white squares.

33

At the start of the Indianapolis 500 auto race, 33 race cars line up in 11 rows of 3, and when the green flag is waved, they're off—traveling much faster than 33 miles per hour! The length of an extra-point kick in the NFL is 33 yards, and in the 1971–72 NBA season, the Los Angeles Lakers won 33 straight games.

The human spine is (usually) made of 33 small bones; the Russian (Cyrillic) alphabet has 33 letters; and Groundhog Day (February 2) is the 33rd day of the year!

SAY IT! WRITE IT!

English: thirty-three
Spanish: treinta y tres
Mandarin: sānshísān
Tagalog: tatlumpu't tatlo

Roman: XXXIII
Babylonian: ⋘𒐗⋘𒐗
Arabic: ٣٣

SHOW ME 33!

$25 + 4 + 4 = 33$

$3 \times 11 = 33$

DO THE MATH!

33 is **odd**.

33 is **composite**.

Factors: 1, 3, 11, and 33

Tens	Ones
3	3

Prime Factorization: 3×11

33 is the difference of two square numbers: $49 - 16 = 33$.

WILD ABOUT 33!

The Alfa Romeo Tipo 33 was an Italian racing car that won a world championship in 1975.

The flag of the United Nations divides the world into 33 sections, including the one at the center—count them!

33
As

Arsenic is the chemical element with atomic number 33. Arsenic is a brittle, semimetallic solid. Arsenic is alloyed with lead for use in car batteries, and with gallium for use in semiconductors. However, arsenic and its compounds are very poisonous.

34

Where can we find the fabulous number 34? Afghanistan is divided into 34 provinces. Porcupines have 34 chromosomes in their cells, and so do sunflowers. U.S. Route 34 reaches an elevation of 12,183 feet in Colorado's Rocky Mountain National Park, making it one of the highest paved highways in the country. And the made-up word *supercalifragilisticexpialidocious* (from the movie *Mary Poppins*) has 34 letters!

DO THE MATH!

34 is **even**. $34 \div 2 = 17$

34 is **composite**.

Factors:
1, 2, 17, and 34

Tens	Ones
3	4

Prime Factorization: 2×17

34 is the sum of two squares: $25 + 9 = 34$.

SHOW ME 34!

$25 + 9 = 34$

$9 + 8 + 9 + 8 = 34$

$36 - 2 = 34$

WILD ABOUT 34!

The world-famous Empire State Building is on 34th Street in New York City. It is 102 stories high—and $102 = 3 \times 34!$

TR 34 AB 1243

In Turkey, if your car's license plate starts with 34, it means you live in Istanbul.

34
Se

Selenium is the chemical element with atomic number 34. The name selenium comes from *Selene*, the name of the ancient Greek goddess of the moon. Selenium is used in fertilizers, glass and ceramics, and solar cells. It is also an essential nutrient; good sources of selenium include Brazil nuts, seafood, and pasta.

100—
90—
80—
70—
60—
50—
40—
● 34
30—
20—
10—
0—

35

The ancient Romans thought 35 was an important number; Roman citizens were divided into 35 tribes for voting purposes. And until recently, almost all movies were recorded using 35-millimeter film. In 2022, a rowing team called Latitude 35 broke a world record by rowing across the Pacific Ocean from California to Hawaii in just under 35 days. And a person must be at least 35 years old to be the president of the United States.

SAY IT! WRITE IT!

English: thirty-five

Spanish: treinta y cinco

French: trente-cinq

Telugu: muppai aidu

Roman: XXXV

Ancient Greek: λε

Hebrew: לה

SHOW ME 35!

$5 \times 7 = 35$

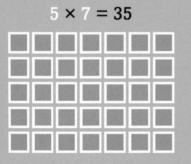

$25 + 10 = 35$

DO THE MATH!

35 is **odd**.

35 is **composite**.

Factors: 1, 5, 7, and 35

Tens	Ones
3	5

Prime Factorization: 5×7

35 is a tetrahedral number because it is the sum of the first 5 triangular numbers: $1 + 3 + 6 + 10 + 15 = 35$.

WILD ABOUT 35!

John F. Kennedy was the 35th president of the United States.

The traditional gift for a 35th wedding anniversary is something made of coral.

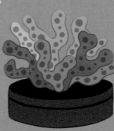

35

Br

Bromine is the chemical element with atomic number 35. Bromine is the only liquid element that is not a metal. It has many uses, including in flameproofing and water purification. The name bromine comes from the Greek *bromos*, meaning "bad smell"!

-100

-90

-80

-70

-60

-50

-40

35 ●

-30

-20

-10

-0

SAY IT! WRITE IT!

English: thirty-six

Spanish: treinta y seis

German: sechsunddreißig

Cantonese: sàamsahpluhk

Roman: XXXVI

Chinese: 三十六

Mayan: ☵

Where have you seen 36 lately? You can see 36 on a yardstick, because there are 36 inches in 1 yard, and on a map, because there are 36 counties in Oregon. There are 36 black keys (and 52 white keys) on a piano. Many early computers featured a 36-bit word length (which is just a unit of data measurement for computers). And the number 36 is very significant in the Jewish religion; the commandment to be kind to strangers is found 36 times in the Torah.

DO THE MATH!

36 is **even**. $36 \div 2 = 18$

36 is **composite**.

Factors: 1, 2, 3, 4, 6, 9, 12, 18, and 36

Tens	Ones
3	6

$36 = 2 \times 18 = 3 \times 12 = 4 \times 9 = 6 \times 6$

Prime Factorization: $2 \times 2 \times 3 \times 3$

36 is both a square number and a triangular number.

SHOW ME 36!

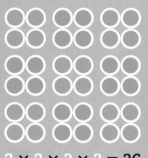

$2 \times 2 \times 3 \times 3 = 36$
$6 \times 6 = 36$

$1 + 2 + 3 + 4 + 5 + 6 + 7 + 8 = 36$

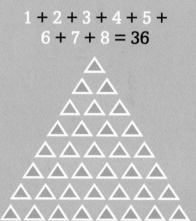

WILD ABOUT 36!

Thirty-Six Views of Mount Fuji is a famous series of prints by the Japanese artist Hokusai. Below is an illustration of one of them, *Thunderstorm Beneath the Summit*.

If two dice numbered 1–6 are rolled, there are 36 possible outcomes, from (1, 1) to (6, 6).

36
Kr

Krypton is the chemical element with atomic number 36. Krypton is a noble gas, which means it doesn't easily combine with other elements. The comic book and movie character Superman is supposed to be from a planet called Krypton.

100 — 90 — 80 — 70 — 60 — 50 — 40 — ●36 — 30 — 20 — 10 — 0

37

The number 37 shows up in the history of aviation—the first flight of Orville Wright in 1903 covered a distance of 37 meters, and in 1909, the first flight across the English Channel (by Louis Blériot) took approximately 37 minutes. The normal human body temperature is about 37 degrees Celsius. And the great English playwright William Shakespeare wrote 37 plays.

SAY IT! WRITE IT!

English: thirty-seven

Spanish: treinta y siete

Mandarin: sānshíqī

Vietnamese: ba mười bảy

Roman: XXXVII

Babylonian: 𐏐𐏐𐏐

Devanagari: ३७

SHOW ME 37!

$$1 + 6 + 12 + 18 = 37$$

37 is prime!

DO THE MATH!

37 is **odd**.

37 is **prime**.

Factors: 1 and 37

Tens	Ones
3	7

37 is the sum of a triangular number and a square number: 21 + 16 = 37.

WILD ABOUT 37!

The Boeing X-37 is a robotic spacecraft operated by the United States Space Force.

Have you ever heard of the Green Monster? It's not something that hides under your bed; it's what baseball fans call the left-field wall in Boston's Fenway Park. It's 37 feet tall, but players still hit home runs over it!

37
Rb

Rubidium is the chemical element with atomic number 37. It used to be considered a rare element, but large deposits have recently been discovered. Rubidium is used in medical imaging and in fireworks to give them a purple color.

100 — 90 — 80 — 70 — 60 — 50 — 40 — 37 — 30 — 20 — 10 — 0

English: thirty-eight

Spanish: treinta y ocho

Haitian Creole: trant uit

Khmer: sam sep pram bei

Roman: XXXVIII

Cistercian: ⅃

Cyrillic: ЛИ

Some numbers, like 38, can be found in the sky—38 Leda is a large asteroid that was discovered in 1856. It is named for the mother of Helen of Troy in Greek mythology. On Earth, 38 is important in Indonesia, which has 38 provinces. Not far from Indonesia, Train 38 is a special express train in Thailand that runs from the Malaysian border to Bangkok. And in the Bible, the Israelites spend 38 years traveling from Kadesh Barnea to the Zered Valley.

DO THE MATH!

38 is **even**. $38 \div 2 = 19$

38 is **composite**.

Factors: 1, 2, 19, and 38

Tens	Ones
3	8

Prime Factorization: 2×19

38 is the sum of two triangular numbers: $28 + 10 = 38$.

38 is the sum of three square numbers: $25 + 9 + 4 = 38$.

SHOW ME 38!

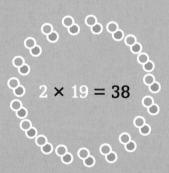

$2 \times 19 = 38$

$25 + 9 + 4 = 38$

WILD ABOUT 38!

LA 38

Louisiana Highway 38 (LA 38) is a state highway in southeastern Louisiana.

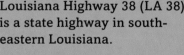

Many animals have 38 chromosomes in each of their cells, including sea otters, raccoons, pigs, lions, tigers—and kitty cats!

38

Sr

Strontium is the chemical element with atomic number 38. Strontium burns with a red flame and is used in fireworks. It is also used in color television sets, toothpaste, and glow-in-the-dark toys.

100 — 90 — 80 — 70 — 60 — 50 — 40 — ●38 — 30 — 20 — 10 — 0

39

Where in the world is 39? *The Thirty-Nine Steps* is a spy novel that has been made into several movies and at least one video game. Plus, "'39" is the name of a song by the English rock band Queen; 39 is the international calling code for Italy; and Washington state has 39 counties. And the Old Testament contains 39 books.

SAY IT! WRITE IT!

English: thirty-nine

Spanish: treinta y nueve

Tagalog: tatlumpu't siyam

Arabic: tis'a wa-thalathun

Roman: XXXIX

Ancient Greek: λθ

Egyptian: ∩∩|||
        ∩ |||

SHOW ME 39!

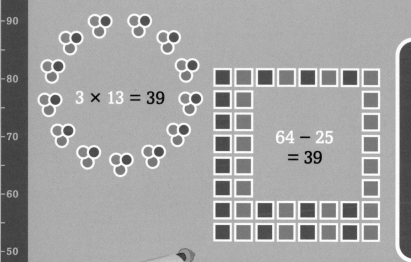

$3 \times 13 = 39$

$64 - 25 = 39$

DO THE MATH!

39 is **odd**.

39 is **composite**.

Factors: 1, 3, 13, and 39

Tens	Ones
3	9

Prime Factorization: 3×13

39 is the difference of two squares: $64 - 25 = 39$.

WILD ABOUT 39!

We the people

Pier 39 is a popular tourist destination in San Francisco.

There were 39 people who signed the United States Constitution in 1787.

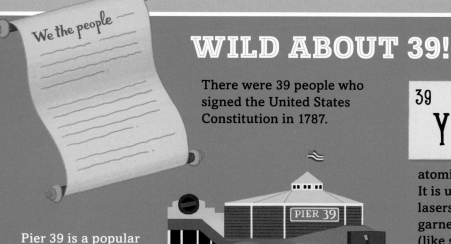

PIER 39

39 **Y**

Yttrium is the chemical element with atomic number 39. It is used to make lasers, synthetic garnets, and (like strontium, element 38) color television sets.

SAY IT! WRITE IT!

English: forty

Spanish: cuarenta

Gujarati: chālīs

Hmong: plaub caug

Roman: XL

Chinese: 四十

Babylonian:

To unlock the secrets of 40, say "Open, Sesame!" That's the magic phrase that opens a cave full of treasure in "Ali Baba and the Forty Thieves." The number 40 appears many times in the Koran and the Bible. Muhammad receives his first revelations from Allah at age 40; Moses spends 40 days on Mount Sinai receiving the Ten Commandments; and rain falls for 40 days and 40 nights during the Biblical Flood. In English, "forty" is the only number word in which the letters are in alphabetical order. And "forty winks" is another term for a nap.

DO THE MATH!

40 is **even**. $40 \div 2 = 20$

40 is **composite**.

Factors: 1, 2, 4, 5, 8, 10, 20, and 40

Tens	Ones
4	0

$40 = 2 \times 20 = 4 \times 10 = 5 \times 8$

Prime Factorization:
$2 \times 2 \times 2 \times 5$

40 is the sum of two squares: $36 + 4 = 40$.

40 is the difference of two squares: $49 - 9 = 40$.

SHOW ME 40!

$36 + 4 = 40$

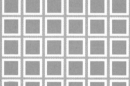

$2 \times 2 \times 2 \times 5 = 40$

$5 \times 8 = 40$

100
90
80
70
60
50
40 ● 40
30
20
10
0

WILD ABOUT 40!

The characters on the popular television show *Sesame Street* like to count, and on November 10, 2009, they counted to 40 for the premiere of the show's 40th season.

In a game of tennis, if you win three points, your score is 40!

40
Zr

Zirconium is the chemical element with atomic number 40. Zirconium is used in nuclear reactors, surgical instruments, jewelry, and lotion to treat poison ivy.

41

If you add the first six prime numbers, you get another prime: 41! The number 41 appears in other places, too. A polygon with 41 sides is called a *tetracontakai-henagon*; 41 is the international calling code for Switzerland; and if you have 1 quarter, 1 dime, 1 nickel, and 1 penny, you have a total of 41 cents!

SHOW ME 41!

$$21 + 20 = 41$$

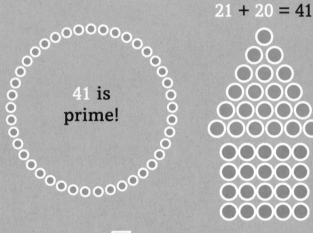

41 is prime!

$$25 + 16 = 41$$

DO THE MATH!

41 is odd.

41 is prime.

Factors: 1 and 41

Tens	Ones
4	1

41 is the sum of two squares: $25 + 16 = 41$.

41 and 43 are twin primes.

WILD ABOUT 41!

In the National Football League's Super Bowl XLI (41), the score of each team was a prime number. The final score was 29 points for the Indianapolis Colts, and 17 points for the Chicago Bears.

41
Nb

Niobium is the chemical element with atomic number 41. It is mainly used in steel alloys that are built into automobiles, jet engines, and even rockets.

42

The number 42 appears in a famous novel called *The Hitchhiker's Guide to the Galaxy*. In the book, a computer named Deep Thought spends seven and half million years finding the answer to the "Ultimate Question of Life, the Universe and Everything." And the answer is . . . 42! The *Gutenberg Bible*, one of the world's first printed books, is called the "42-line Bible" because there are 42 lines printed on each page. And Tower 42 is a skyscraper in London, England, named for its 42 cantilevered floors (meaning they're supported only at one end).

DO THE MATH!

42 is **even**. $42 \div 2 = 21$

42 is **composite**.

Factors: 1, 2, 3, 6, 7, 14, 21, and 42

Tens	Ones
4	2

$42 = 2 \times 21 = 3 \times 14 = 6 \times 7$

Prime Factorization: $2 \times 3 \times 7$

42 is twice a triangular number: $2 \times 21 = 42$.

SHOW ME 42!

$6 \times 7 = 42$

$21 + 21 = 42$

WILD ABOUT 42!

Jackie Robinson

Jackie Robinson was the first African American player in the modern era of Major League Baseball. His uniform number was 42.

In the book *Alice's Adventures in Wonderland* (which has 42 illustrations), the King invents Rule 42, which is "All persons more than a mile high to leave the court."

42
Mo

Molybdenum is the chemical element with atomic number 42. We need small amounts of molybdenum in our bodies—and fortunately most people get plenty in their diet.

43

Have you seen 43 out in the world lately? John F. Kennedy was 43 years old when he was elected in 1960; he was the youngest person ever elected president. The children's TV show *Odd Squad* features the number 43, which is the shorthand for the villain, Odd Todd. And the peripheral nervous system in the human body has 43 pairs of nerves.

SHOW ME 43!

43 is prime!

$$25 + 9 + 9 = 43$$

DO THE MATH!

43 is **odd**.

43 is **prime**.

Factors: 1 and 43

Tens	Ones
4	3

43 is the sum of three squares: 25 + 9 + 9 = 43.

41 and 43 are twin primes.

WILD ABOUT 43!

"Sonnet 43" is a famous poem by Elizabeth Barrett Browning. It begins like this:

How do I love thee?
Let me count the ways.

The Ha'penny Bridge is a famous bridge in Dublin, Ireland. It is approximately 43 meters in length.

43
Tc

Technetium is the chemical element with atomic number 43. Technetium was the first artificially produced element. It is radioactive and essentially nonexistent on Earth.

You might not realize it, but 44 is all around us. The Forty Fours is a group of islands near New Zealand in the South Pacific Ocean. The islands are likely named for their latitude, which is very close to 44 degrees south. A total of 44 candles are lit to celebrate the eight nights of the Jewish winter holiday of Hanukkah. And *44 Cats* is an animated children's television series in Italy. In Italian, you would say *Quarantaquattro gatti*!

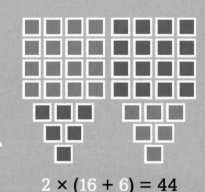

DO THE MATH!

44 is **even**. $44 \div 2 = 22$

44 is **composite**.

Factors:
1, 2, 4, 11, 22, and 44

Tens	Ones
4	4

$44 = 2 \times 22 = 4 \times 11$

Prime Factorization:
$2 \times 2 \times 11$

44 is the sum of a triangular and a square number: $28 + 16 = 44$.

SHOW ME 44!

$28 + 16 = 44$

$2 \times (16 + 6) = 44$

WILD ABOUT 44!

INTERSTATE 44

Interstate 44 is a major highway that runs for about 634 miles from Wichita Falls, Texas, to St. Louis, Missouri.

Forty-Four is a small community in Arkansas. It was supposedly named for the 44 people who signed the petition to get a post office.

44
Ru

Ruthenium is the chemical element with atomic number 44. It is used in jet engines, electronics, and jewelry.

●44

45

You can find 45 in space—45 Eugenia is a large asteroid that has at least two moons. On Earth, a latitude of 45 degrees north is halfway between the equator and the North Pole, and 45 degrees south is halfway between the equator and the South Pole.

A soccer match consists of two periods that each last 45 minutes; 45 is the international calling code for Denmark; and Forty-Five is the name of a popular card game that originated in Ireland!

SHOW ME 45!

$$3 \times 3 \times 5 = 45$$

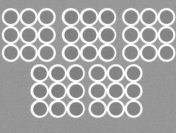

$$1 + 2 + 3 + 4 + 5 + 6 + 7 + 8 + 9 = 45$$

HOLLYWOOD

DO THE MATH!

45 is **odd**.

45 is **composite**.

Factors:
1, 3, 5, 9, 15, and 45

Tens	Ones
4	5

$45 = 3 \times 15 = 5 \times 9$

Prime Factorization:
$3 \times 3 \times 5$

45 is a triangular number:
$1 + 2 + 3 + \ldots + 8 + 9 = 45$.

45 is the sum of two squares: $36 + 9 = 45$.

Each letter in the famous "Hollywood" sign in the Hollywood Hills of Southern California is 45 feet tall.

WILD ABOUT 45!

Your grandparents probably listened to music by playing records called 45s because they spun around 45 times per minute on a record player. A 45 plays just one song per side!

45
Rh

Rhodium is the chemical element with atomic number 45. It is used in jewelry, as a catalyst, and in alloys with platinum and palladium.

—100
—90
—80
—70
—60
—50
45●
—40
—30
—20
—10
—0

46

SAY IT! WRITE IT!

English: forty-six

Spanish: cuarenta y seis

French: quarante-six

Japanese: yon-jū roku

Roman: XLVI

Cherokee: ᎤᏑᏓᎵ ᏔᎵᏏ

Egyptian: ∩∩|||
∩∩|||

If you're from South Carolina, you might know that your state has 46 counties! Where else does 46 appear? There are normally 46 chromosomes (in 23 pairs) in each cell of the human body. In modern Japanese, the hiragana and katakana alphabets each contain 46 letters. And in the year 46 BCE, the Roman empire switched from the Roman calendar to the Julian calendar, which meant that the year 46 BCE had 445 days!

DO THE MATH!

46 is **even**. $46 \div 2 = 23$

46 is **composite**.

Factors: 1, 2, 23, and 46

Tens	Ones
4	6

Prime Factorization: 2×23

46 is the sum of three consecutive triangular numbers: $10 + 15 + 21 = 46$.

SHOW ME 46!

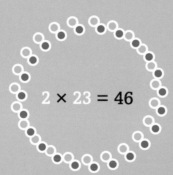

$2 \times 23 = 46$

$36 + 10 = 46$

WILD ABOUT 46!

Valentino Rossi is a retired Italian motorcycle racer who is considered one of the best of all time. He rode with the number 46 for his entire career.

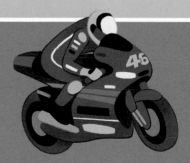

The "46 High Peaks" are a famous group of 46 mountain peaks in the Adirondack Mountains in New York. People who have climbed all 46 peaks are called "Forty-Sixers."

46
Pd

Palladium is the chemical element with atomic number 46. It has many uses, including in watches, surgical instruments, dental fillings, and jewelry.

47

Traveling across the Pacific Ocean, we find that Japan is divided into 47 prefectures (similar to states). Continuing on to Africa, we see that Kenya is divided into 47 counties. And up north in Norway, the international calling code is—you guessed it—47!

SHOW ME 47!

47 is prime!

$$25 + 9 + 9 + 4 = 47$$

DO THE MATH!

47 is **odd**.

47 is **prime**.

Factors: 1 and 47

Tens	Ones
4	7

47 is the sum of four squares: 25 + 9 + 9 + 4 = 47.

WILD ABOUT 47!

A total of 47 piglets were used in the filming of the movie *Babe*: 46 real piglets plus 1 robotic piglet!

A modern harp typically has 47 strings.

47

Ag

Silver is the chemical element with atomic number 47. Its symbol, Ag, comes from *argentum*, its name in Latin. Silver has been used and valued by humans for thousands of years. It has a great many uses, including in jewelry, mirrors, silverware, batteries, and coins.

English: forty-eight

Spanish: cuarenta y ocho

Mandarin: sìshíbā

German: achtundvierzig

Roman: XLVIII

Ancient Greek: μη

Thai: ๔๘

Mathematically speaking, 48 is the smallest number with 10 factors. In the nonmath world, 48 appears in Judaism, where there are 48 ways to acquire wisdom. And in Buddhism, a monk named Dharmakara is said to have made 48 great vows to provide ultimate salvation to countless beings.

The German composer Johann Sebastian Bach is famous for the *Well-Tempered Clavier*, a collection of 48 compositions for keyboard instruments. An NBA basketball game is divided into 4 quarters of 12 minutes each, for a total of 48 minutes. And Alaskans refer to the 48 contiguous states as the "Lower 48."

DO THE MATH!

48 is **even.** $48 \div 2 = 24$

48 is **composite.**

Factors: 1, 2, 3, 4, 6, 8, 12, 16, 24, and 48

Tens	Ones
4	8

$48 = 2 \times 24 = 3 \times 16 = 4 \times 12 = 6 \times 8$

Prime Factorization: $2 \times 2 \times 2 \times 2 \times 3$

64 is the difference of two square numbers: $64 - 16 = 48$.

64 is also 3 times a square: $3 \times 16 = 48$.

SHOW ME 48!

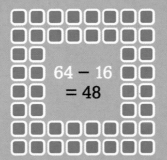

$64 - 16 = 48$

$$2 \times 2 \times 2 \times 2 \times 3 = 48$$

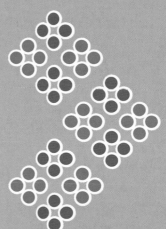

WILD ABOUT 48!

The ancient Greeks named 48 constellations in the night sky. You might recognize the Big Dipper in this picture, but it's part of a larger constellation called Ursa Major (the Great Bear).

48
Cd

Cadmium is the chemical element with atomic number 48. It has many uses, including in batteries, televisions, semiconductors, paint pigments, and electroplating steel.

The U.S. flag had 48 stars from 1912 until 1959 (when Alaska and Hawaii joined the Union). Notice that the flag had 6 rows of 8 stars, and as we know, $6 \times 8 = 48$!

Meet 49—seven sevens! The square number 49 shows up wherever you see a 7 by 7 square, because 7 × 7 = 49. For example, the game called Lasca is a variation of checkers that is played on a 7 by 7 board with 49 squares. According to the Buddhist religion, Siddhartha Gautama (who is now known as the Buddha) sits under the bodhi tree meditating for 49 days before experiencing enlightenment. Finally, Rocky Marciano was a heavyweight boxer with a perfect record—49 wins in 49 professional bouts!

SHOW ME 49!

7 × 7 = 49

28 + 21 = 49

DO THE MATH!

49 is **odd**.

49 is **composite**.

Factors: 1, 7, and 49

Tens	Ones
4	9

Prime Factorization: 7 × 7

49 is the sum of two triangular numbers: 28 + 21 = 49.

WILD ABOUT 49!

The term "forty-niners" describes people who participated in the California Gold Rush of 1849. And "49ers" is the name of the National Football League team from San Francisco.

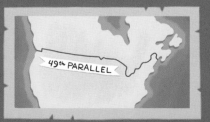

The 49th parallel of latitude makes up about 1,260 miles of the border between the United States and Canada.

49 In

Indium is the chemical element with atomic number 49. It is used in transistors and other electrical components, in LCD screens, and to make mirrors.

SAY IT! WRITE IT!

English: fifty

Spanish: cincuenta

Vietnamese: năm mươi

Tamil: aimpatu

Roman: L

Ge'ez: ፶

Egyptian: ∩∩∩ ∩∩

Let's talk about fabulous 50—halfway to 100! If you have 2 quarters, or 5 dimes, or 10 nickels, you have 50 cents—half of a dollar. And if you're lucky, you might have a $50 bill!

More about 50: The first book of the Bible, Genesis, has 50 chapters, and the Christian holiday of Pentecost takes place 50 days after Easter. In darts, the bull's-eye in the center of the dartboard is worth 50 points. And 50 percent equals one half; if we decide to share a box of cookies equally, we might say "Let's split them fifty-fifty"—meaning 50 percent each.

DO THE MATH!

50 is **even**. 50 ÷ 2 = 25

50 is **composite**.

Factors:
1, 2, 5, 10, 25, and 50

Tens	Ones
5	0

$50 = 2 \times 25 = 5 \times 10$

Prime Factorization: $2 \times 5 \times 5$

50 is twice a square number: $2 \times 25 = 50$.

SHOW ME 50!

$2 \times 25 = 50$

$5 \times 10 = 50$

$25 + 16 + 9 = 50$

The 50 states in the United States are represented by 50 stars on the U.S. flag. The stars are arranged in 5 rows of 6 stars plus 4 rows of 5 stars. Since $(5 \times 6) + (4 \times 5) = 50$, it works!

WILD ABOUT 50!

The 50th wedding anniversary is called the "Golden Anniversary" because the traditional gift for a 50th anniversary is something made of gold.

50

Sn

Tin is the chemical element with atomic number 50. We have known of tin since ancient times; its symbol, "Sn," comes from *stannum*, the Latin name for tin. It's a silvery-white, malleable metal with many uses; for example, bronze is an alloy of tin and copper. But nowadays, "tin cans" are usually made of aluminum!

100
90
80
70
60
50 ● 50
40
30
20
10
0

51

During the years 1787–1788, 51 was an important number. That's when Founding Father Alexander Hamilton wrote 51 essays as part of the Federalist Papers, which defended the U.S. Constitution. And 51 came up again in 1945, when 51 countries came together to form the United Nations.

SHOW ME 51!

$3 \times 17 = 51$

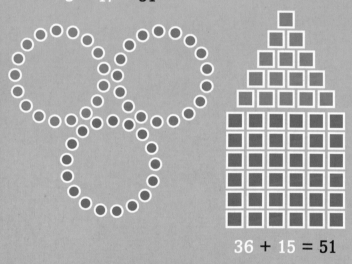

$36 + 15 = 51$

DO THE MATH!

51 is **odd**.

51 is **composite**.

Factors: 1, 3, 17, and 51

Tens	Ones
5	1

Prime Factorization: 3×17

51 is the sum of a square number and a triangular number: $36 + 15 = 51$.

51 is the difference of two squares: $100 - 49 = 51$.

WILD ABOUT 51!

51 Pegasi b, also known as Dimidium, was one of the first planets discovered outside of our solar system.

51 Sb

Antimony is the chemical element with atomic number 51. In ancient Egypt, antimony was used for black eye makeup!

SAY IT! WRITE IT!

English: fifty-two

Spanish: cincuenta y dos

Mandarin: wǔshíèr

Punjabi: bavanja

Roman: LII

Ancient Greek: νβ

Arabic: ٥٢

Where can we find 52? Well, Abraham Lincoln was 52 years old when he became the U.S. president in 1861. The Mayan and Aztec calendars were both based on a cycle that repeated every 52 years, and in our calendar, 1 year is approximately 52 weeks. Also, 52 is the nickname of a mysterious whale that lives somewhere in the Pacific Ocean; it "sings" at a frequency of 52 hertz, unlike other whales.

DO THE MATH!

52 is **even**. $52 \div 2 = 26$

52 is **composite**.

Factors:
1, 2, 4, 13, 26, and 52

Tens	Ones
5	2

$52 = 2 \times 26 = 4 \times 13$

Prime Factorization:
$2 \times 2 \times 13$

52 is the sum of two squares: $36 + 16 = 52$.

52 is the sum of a cube number and a square number: $27 + 25 = 52$.

SHOW ME 52!

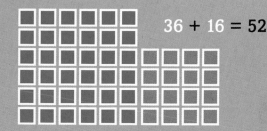

$36 + 16 = 52$

$21 + 10 + 21 = 52$

WILD ABOUT 52!

Have you ever played 52 Pickup? To play the game, you take a standard pack of 52 playing cards, scatter them all over the floor, and yell "52 pickup!" And then someone has to pick up all 52 cards.

There are 52 white keys and 36 black keys on a full-sized piano keyboard, for a total of 88 keys.

52
Te

Tellurium is the chemical element with atomic number 52. It is used as a coloring agent in ceramics.

100 —
90 —
80 —
70 —
60 —
• 52
50 —
40 —
30 —
20 —
10 —
0 —

53

In the Dr. Seuss book *How the Grinch Stole Christmas*, the Grinch complains that he's been listening to the Whos celebrate Christmas for 53 years. North Dakota has 53 counties; in the trucking industry, semi-trucks often pull 53-foot trailers; and a polygon with 53 sides is called a *pentacontatrigon*!

SHOW ME 53!

49 + 4 = 53

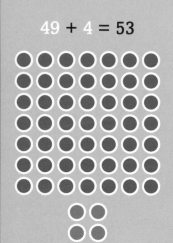

53 is prime!

DO THE MATH!

53 is **odd**.

53 is **prime**.

Factors: 1 and 53

Tens	Ones
5	3

53 is the sum of two squares: 49 + 4 = 53.

53 is the sum of a triangular number and a square number: 28 + 25 = 53.

WILD ABOUT 53!

HERBIE

53 is the number on Herbie, the Volkswagen Beetle car in several Disney movies, beginning with *The Love Bug* in 1968.

A crater on the Moon named Tycho is 53 miles across.

53

I

Iodine is the chemical element with atomic number 53. It is useful in medicine, photography, animal feeds, printing inks, and dyes.

100
90
80
70
60
53
50
40
30
20
10
0

SAY IT! WRITE IT!

English: fifty-four

Spanish: cincuenta y cuatro

Hawaiian: kanalimakūmāhā

Armenian: hisunch'vors

Roman: LIV

Chinese: 五十四

Egyptian: ∩∩∩ ∩∩ IIII

Looking to space, 54 Alexandra is an asteroid that was discovered in 1858. The 54-mile march from Selma to Montgomery, Alabama, in 1965 was an important milestone in the Civil Rights Movement. And if you include the two jokers, there are 54 cards in a deck of cards!

DO THE MATH!

54 is **even.** $54 \div 2 = 27$

54 is **composite.**

Factors: 1, 2, 3, 6, 9, 18, 27, and 54

Tens	Ones
5	4

$54 = 2 \times 27 = 3 \times 18 = 6 \times 9$

Prime Factorization: $2 \times 3 \times 3 \times 3$

54 is twice a cube number: $2 \times 27 = 54$.

SHOW ME 54!

$2 \times 3 \times 3 \times 3 = 54$

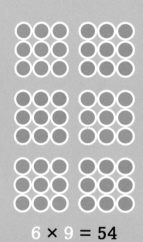

$6 \times 9 = 54$

WILD ABOUT 54!

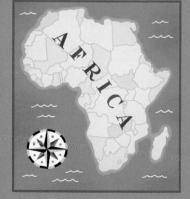

There are 54 countries in Africa, from Algeria to Zimbabwe.

There are 54 colored squares on a Rubik's Cube. There are 9 squares on each face, and a cube has 6 faces—and $6 \times 9 = 54$.

54 Xe

Xenon is the chemical element with atomic number 54. Xenon is used in very bright lamps for deep-sea exploration, and by NASA as a propellant for spacecraft. And it's the only chemical element whose name starts with X!

100
90
80
70
60
●54
50
40
30
20
10
0

In the game of Bingo, 55 has the nickname "Snakes Alive." (That rhymes with "fifty-five," and the two 5s look a little like snakes!) Did you know that the state of West Virginia has 55 counties? And NCAA basketball rules don't allow the digits 6, 7, 8, or 9 to be used for a uniform number, so the highest possible uniform number is 55!

SAY IT! WRITE IT!

English: fifty-five

Spanish: cincuenta y cinco

French: cinquante-cinq

Telugu: yābhai aidu

Roman: LV

Mayan: ··
‗‗‗

Hebrew: נה

SHOW ME 55!

$$64 - 9 = 55$$

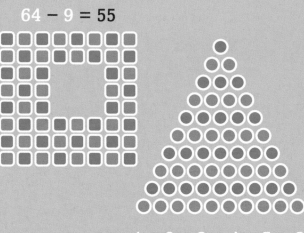

$$1 + 2 + 3 + 4 + 5 + 6 + 7 + 8 + 9 + 10 = 55$$

DO THE MATH!

55 is **odd**.

55 is **composite**.

Factors: 1, 5, 11, and 55

Tens	Ones
5	5

Prime Factorization: 5×11

55 is a triangular number: $1 + 2 + 3 + \ldots + 9 + 10 = 55$.

55 is a square pyramidal number because $1 + 4 + 9 + 16 + 25 = 55$. You could build a pyramid with square layers of 1, 4, 9, 16, and 25 spheres.

WILD ABOUT 55!

This is hexagram 55 from the *I Ching*. It is named "fēng," which means "abundance" or "fullness."

The Bugatti Type 55 was a sports car produced from 1932 to 1935.

55 Cs

Cesium is the chemical element with atomic number 55. Cesium is a silvery-gold metal that melts at 83 degrees Fahrenheit, so it would be a liquid on a hot day.

56

SAY IT! WRITE IT!

English: fifty-six

Spanish: cincuenta y seis

Mandarin: wǔshíliù

Arabic: sitta wa-khamsun

Roman: LVI

Cistercian: ٦'

Devanagari: ५६

Fifty-Six is the name of a small town in Arkansas; 56 people signed the U.S. Declaration of Independence; the ancient Greek philosopher Aristotle believed that the universe was divided into 56 layers; and the famous child actor Shirley Temple always had exactly 56 curls in her hair!

DO THE MATH!

56 is **even**. $56 \div 2 = 28$

56 is **composite**.

Factors: 1, 2, 4, 7, 8, 14, 28, and 56

Tens	Ones
5	6

$56 = 2 \times 28 = 4 \times 14 = 7 \times 8$

Prime Factorization: $2 \times 2 \times 2 \times 7$

56 is the difference of two squares: $81 - 25 = 56$.

56 is a tetrahedral number because $1 + 3 + 6 + 10 + 15 + 21 = 56$.

SHOW ME 56!

$2 \times 2 \times 2 \times 7 = 56$

$28 + 28 = 56$

WILD ABOUT 56!

In 1941, Joe DiMaggio of the New York Yankees got at least one hit in 56 consecutive games, a record that still stands.

56

Ba

Barium is the chemical element with atomic number 56. It has many uses, including in paint, glassmaking, and X-ray imaging.

Scientists in Australia recently discovered 56 new species of arachnids called *schizomids*, most of which live their entire lives underground.

Four out of the first six U.S. presidents (George Washington, Thomas Jefferson, James Madison, and John Quincy Adams) were 57 years of age when they took office. In 1970, the Norwegian explorer Thor Heyerdahl took 57 days to cross the Atlantic Ocean in a reed papyrus boat. One57 is a 1,005-foot-tall skyscraper on 57th Street in New York City. And the Maybach 57 was a German luxury car that cost over $300,000.

SHOW ME 57!

$$36 + 21 = 57$$

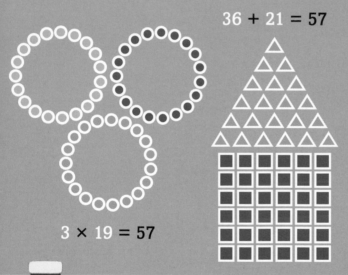

$$3 \times 19 = 57$$

DO THE MATH!

57 is **odd**.

57 is **composite**.

Factors: 1, 3, 19, and 57

Tens	Ones
5	7

Prime Factorization: 3×19

57 is the sum of three squares: $25 + 16 + 16 = 57$.

57 is the sum of a square and a triangular number: $36 + 21 = 57$.

WILD ABOUT 57!

57 is on every bottle of Heinz ketchup. Heinz has been using the slogan "57 Varieties" for over 100 years; the number was supposed to represent the number of types of food the company produced.

The constellation Pisces includes an elliptical galaxy called NGC 57!

57

La

Lanthanum is the chemical element with atomic number 57. It has many uses, including in rechargeable batteries for hybrid cars, electron microscopes, and night-vision goggles.

100
90
80
70
60
57
50
40
30
20
10
0

58

SAY IT! WRITE IT!

English: fifty-eight

Spanish: cincuenta y ocho

Vietnamese: năm mươi tám

Haitian Creole: senkant uit

Roman: LVIII

Chinese: 五十八

Egyptian: ∩∩∩||||
         ∩∩ ||||

There are dozens of highways numbered 58 in the United States alone. One of them is U.S. Route 58, which runs over 500 miles from Tennessee to Virginia. *Fifty-Eight* is a musical composition by the famous composer John Cage; he composed it to be played by 58 musicians in the 58 archways of a building in Austria. And on the TV show *SpongeBob SquarePants*, the character Patrick declares "58 is, like, the luckiest number ever!"

DO THE MATH!

58 is **even**. 58 ÷ 2 = 29

58 is **composite**.

Factors: 1, 2, 29, and 58

Tens	Ones
5	8

Prime Factorization: 2 × 29

58 is the sum of the first 7 prime numbers: 2 + 3 + 5 + 7 + 11 + 13 + 17 = 58.

58 is the sum of two squares: 49 + 9 = 58.

SHOW ME 58!

49 + 9 = 58

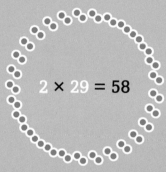

2 × 29 = 58

WILD ABOUT 58!

In 2019, a team of people in Germany built the world's largest sandcastle at the time, which was almost 58 feet tall.

There are 58 stars that sailors commonly use to help navigate at sea during the nighttime.

58
Ce

Cerium is the chemical element with atomic number 58. Cerium is named for the asteroid (or dwarf planet) Ceres.

100 — 90 — 80 — 70 — 60 — ●58 — 50 — 40 — 30 — 20 — 10 — 0

59

In 1965, Satchel Paige became the oldest Major League Baseball player at age 59. In the 1970s, many feminists wore buttons with "59¢" on them, drawing attention to reports that women earned 59 cents for every dollar earned by an equally qualified man. And it takes Saturn about 59 years to go around the Sun twice!

SHOW ME 59!

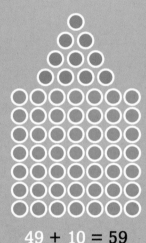

49 + 10 = 59

25 + 9 + 25 = 59

DO THE MATH!

59 is **odd**.

59 is **prime**.

Factors:
1 and 59 only

Tens	Ones
5	9

59 is the sum of three consecutive primes: 17 + 19 + 23 = 59.

59 and 61 are twin primes.

WILD ABOUT 59!

It takes about 59 days for the planet Mercury to spin around once on its axis.

59
Pr

Praseodymium is the chemical element with atomic number 59. Praseodymium is a rare earth metal that is used (like cerium, element 58) in bright lights for the motion picture industry. It is also alloyed with magnesium and used in aircraft engines.

Catholics often pray using a rosary, which traditionally contains 59 beads (53 "Hail Mary" beads plus 6 "Our Father" beads).

SAY IT! WRITE IT!

English: sixty

Spanish: sesenta

Mandarin: liùshí

Greek: exínta

Roman: LX

Khmer: ៦០

Tamil: சு௦

The number 60 was important to the ancient Babylonians, who used a base-60 number system, probably because 60 has so many factors. We still use base-60 in our measurement of time: There are 60 seconds in 1 minute, and 60 minutes in 1 hour. And each angle of an equilateral triangle measures 60 degrees.

DO THE MATH!

60 is **even**. $60 \div 2 = 30$

60 is **composite**.

Factors:
1, 2, 3, 4, 5, 6, 10, 12, 15, 20, 30, and 60

Tens	Ones
6	0

$60 = 2 \times 30 = 3 \times 20 = 4 \times 15 = 5 \times 12 = 6 \times 10$

Prime Factorization:
$2 \times 2 \times 3 \times 5$

60 is the smallest number to have 12 or more factors.

60 is the sum of two triangular numbers: $45 + 15 = 60$.

SHOW ME 60!

$45 + 15 = 60$

$2 \times 2 \times 3 \times 5 = 60$

WILD ABOUT 60!

The game Sternhalma uses 60 marbles; at the start of the game, these marbles are arranged into 6 triangles with 10 marbles each. Notice that the 61 empty spaces in the middle form a centered hexagon.

There are four special solid figures called *Archimedean solids* that each have exactly 60 vertices. Here's one of them, the *rhombicosidodecahedron*.

60

Nd

Neodymium is the chemical element with atomic number 60.

It is a component in special types of glass that are used in welding goggles, lasers, and astronomical instruments.

61

Check a map to find number 61! U.S. Route 61 is a major U.S. highway that travels 1,400 miles from Minnesota to Louisiana. It is called the "Blues Highway" because of its connection with blues music, and it inspired the album *Highway 61 Revisited* by Bob Dylan.

The 61st book of the Bible has 61 verses; 61 is the number of points required to win a game of cribbage; Roger Maris hit 61 home runs in 1961, breaking Babe Ruth's record; the Snellen chart used to test vision has a total of 61 letters; and an episode of *Jeopardy!* has a total of 61 questions and answers.

SHOW ME 61!

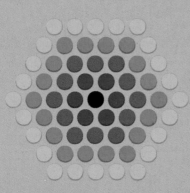

$$1 + 6 + 12 + 18 + 24 = 61$$

$$36 + 25 = 61$$

DO THE MATH!

61 is **odd**.

61 is **prime**.

Factors: 1 and 61

	Tens	Ones
	6	1

59 and 61 are twin primes.

61 is the sum of two squares: $36 + 25 = 61$.

WILD ABOUT 61!

On the island of Borneo, there are (at least) 61 species of rats and mice.

61
Pm

Promethium is the chemical element with atomic number 61. Promethium is a radioactive metal that does not appear to exist on Earth but is apparently produced in some stars. This element is named for Prometheus, a Titan god of fire in Greek mythology.

SAY IT! WRITE IT!

English: sixty-two

Spanish: sesenta y dos

Korean: yesun dul

Bengali: bāṣaṭṭi

Roman: LXII

Ancient Greek: ξβ

Chinese: 六十二

Donkeys have 62 chromosomes in each cell, and so do spongy moths. The international calling code for Indonesia is 62. And in 1998, Mark McGwire hit his 62nd home run on September 8, breaking Roger Maris's record—then Sammy Sosa hit his own 62nd home run on September 13. There's also a solid figure with 62 faces called a *rhombicosidodecahedron*. Try to say that 62 times fast!

DO THE MATH!

62 is **even**. $62 \div 2 = 31$

62 is **composite**.

Factors: 1, 2, 31, and 62

Tens	Ones
6	2

Prime Factorization: 2×31

62 is the sum of three cube numbers: $27 + 27 + 8 = 62$.

SHOW ME 62!

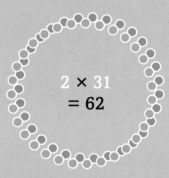

$2 \times 31 = 62$

$49 + 9 + 4 = 62$

WILD ABOUT 62!

Liechtenstein is one of the smallest countries in Europe, with a total area of 62 square miles.

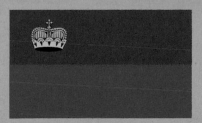

BINGO

15	20	38	58	62
4	22	41	66	70
8	19	53		75
11				51
9				

For the number 62 in a Bingo game, callers often shout "Tickety-boo!"

62 **Sm**

Samarium is the chemical element with atomic number 62. It is used in headphones, small motors, and electric guitar pickups.

100 — 90 — 80 — 70 — ●62 60 — 50 — 40 — 30 — 20 — 10 — 0

63

A scientist recently counted 63 species of mosquito in Georgia. Do you think there are 63 different kinds of mosquito bites? Michael Jordan scored an NBA playoff record of 63 points in a game in 1986. Queen Victoria ruled the United Kingdom for over 63 years. And a *hogshead* is a liquid measure that (usually) equals 63 gallons.

SHOW ME 63!

$$3 \times 3 \times 7 = 63$$

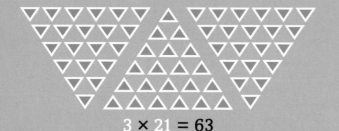

$$3 \times 21 = 63$$

DO THE MATH!

63 is **odd**.

63 is **composite**.

Factors:
1, 3, 7, 9, 21, and 63

Tens	Ones
6	3

$$63 = 3 \times 21 = 7 \times 9$$

Prime Factorization:
$3 \times 3 \times 7$

63 is the difference of two squares: $64 - 1 = 63$.

63 is three times a triangular number: $3 \times 21 = 63$.

WILD ABOUT 63!

The total length of a bowling lane is approximately 63 feet.

In old English currency, 1 *guinea* was worth 21 *shillings*, and 1 shilling was worth 3 *groats*—so 1 guinea was worth 63 groats!

63 Eu *Europium* is the chemical element with atomic number 63. Europium is named for—you'll never guess—Europe!

SAY IT! WRITE IT!

English: sixty-four

Spanish: sesenta y cuatro

Mandarin: liùshísì

Gujarati: chosaṭh

Roman: LXIV

Mayan: ··
         ····

Armenian: ԿԴ

If you start with 1 and keep doubling, you get 1, 2, 4, 8, 16, 32, and then: 64! In measurements, 64 fluid ounces equals 1 half-gallon, or 2 quarts. In Hinduism, the god Shiva is said to appear in 64 forms. The ancient Chinese text called the *I Ching* contains 64 hexagrams that are used for fortune-telling. "When I'm Sixty-Four" was a popular song by the Beatles. And the Commodore 64 was a popular home computer introduced in 1982.

DO THE MATH!

64 is **even**. $64 \div 2 = 32$

64 is **composite**.

Factors: 1, 2, 4, 8, 16, 32, and 64

Tens	Ones
6	4

$64 = 2 \times 32 = 4 \times 16 = 8 \times 8$

Prime Factorization:
$2 \times 2 \times 2 \times 2 \times 2 \times 2$

64 is a square number (because it equals 8×8), a cube number (because it equals $4 \times 4 \times 4$), and a 6th power (because it equals $2 \times 2 \times 2 \times 2 \times 2 \times 2$).

64 is the difference of two squares: $100 - 36 = 64$.

SHOW ME 64!

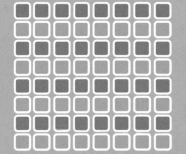

$8 \times 8 = 64$

$2 \times 2 \times 2 \times 2 \times 2 \times 2 = 64$

WILD ABOUT 64!

There are 64 colors in many standard packages of crayons.

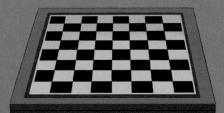

The games of chess and checkers are both played on a board with 64 squares (in 8 rows of 8 squares).

64

Gd

Gadolinium is the chemical element with atomic number 64. Gadolinium is used in the manufacturing of television sets.

65

The age for retirement in many countries is 65. Chicken 65 is a spicy, deep-fried chicken dish that originated in India. Elizabeth Taylor wore 65 different costumes for her starring role in the movie *Cleopatra*. And in German, the number 777,777 can be written as a single long word—*siebenhundertsiebenundsiebzigtausendsiebenhundertsiebenundsiebzig*—which has 65 letters!

SAY IT! WRITE IT!

English: sixty-five

Spanish: sesenta y cinco

Vietnamese: sáu mươi lăm

Arabic: khamsa wa-sittun

Roman: LXV

Babylonian: 𒐕 𒐙

Chinese: 六十五

SHOW ME 65!

$$49 + 16 = 65$$

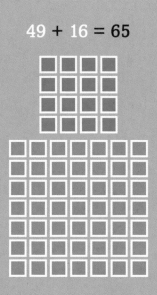

$$5 \times 13 = 65$$

DO THE MATH!

65 is **odd**.

65 is **composite**.

Factors: 1, 5, 13, and 65

Tens	Ones
6	5

Prime Factorization: 5×13

65 is the sum of two squares: $64 + 1 = 65$ and $49 + 16 = 65$.

65 is the difference of two squares: $81 - 16 = 65$.

WILD ABOUT 65!

The traditional gift for a 65th wedding anniversary is blue sapphire.

65 **Tb**

Terbium is the chemical element with atomic number 65. Terbium is used to help make the green color in television sets.

A recent study counted 65 animal species that have their own form of laughter. These species include cows, seals, dogs, and rats.

SAY IT! WRITE IT!

English: sixty-six

Spanish: sesenta y seis

Portuguese: sessenta e seis

Hindi: chhiyaasath

Roman: LXVI

Ancient Greek: ξϛ

Egyptian: ∩∩|||
∩∩|||

In 2021, Justin Tucker from the Baltimore Ravens broke the National Football League record for longest field goal with a 66-yard kick. Sixty-Six is the name of a popular card game that began in Germany; in German, you would call it *Sechsundsechzig*. And the Protestant Bible has a total of 66 books.

DO THE MATH!

66 is **even**. $66 \div 2 = 33$

66 is **composite**.

Factors: 1, 2, 3, 6, 11, 22, 33, and 66

Tens	Ones
6	6

$66 = 2 \times 33 = 3 \times 22 = 6 \times 11$

Prime Factorization: $2 \times 3 \times 11$

66 is a triangular number: $1 + 2 + 3 + 4 + 5 + 6 + 7 + 8 + 9 + 10 + 11 = 66$.

66 is the sum of three squares: $25 + 25 + 16 = 66$.

SHOW ME 66!

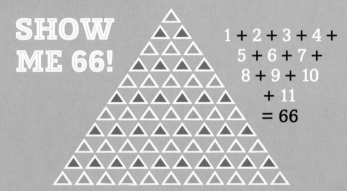

$1 + 2 + 3 + 4 + 5 + 6 + 7 + 8 + 9 + 10 + 11 = 66$

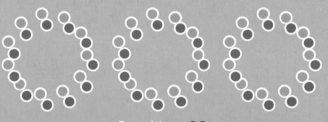

$6 \times 11 = 66$
$2 \times 3 \times 11 = 66$

WILD ABOUT 66!

ROUTE 66

Route 66 was one of the first highways in the United States. It was established in 1926 and originally ran from Chicago, Illinois, to Santa Monica, California. Route 66 (sometimes called "The Main Street of America") is a famous highway that is much recognized in popular culture.

The Spanish Grand Prix is a car race in which cars make 66 laps around this track:

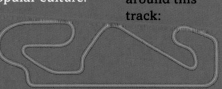

66 Dy

Dysprosium is the chemical element with atomic number 66. It has been used to make lasers in combination with vanadium (element 23).

● 66

67

There are 67 inches in 1 *smoot*, a humorous unit of length named for college student Oliver R. Smoot in Boston in 1958. (Oliver R. Smoot was 67 inches tall.) A polygon with 67 sides is called a *hexacontaheptagon*. And just in case, you should know that it's possible to cut a pizza into 67 pieces with just 11 straight cuts!

SAY IT! WRITE IT!

English: sixty-seven

Spanish: sesenta y siete

Italian: sessantasette

Persian (Farsi): shast o haft

———————————

Roman: LXVII

Bengali: ৬৭

Thai: ๖๗

SHOW ME 67!

$$36 + 21 + 10 = 67$$

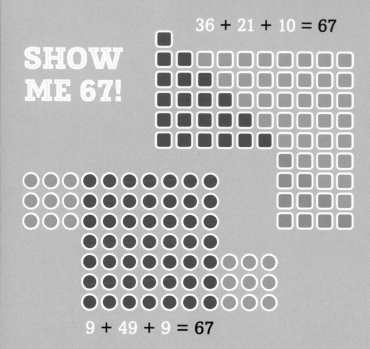

$$9 + 49 + 9 = 67$$

DO THE MATH!

67 is **odd**.

67 is prime.

Tens	Ones
6	7

Factors: 1 and 67

67 is the sum of five consecutive primes: $7 + 11 + 13 + 17 + 19 = 67$.

67 is approximately two-thirds of 100. (The exact value is 66.66666 . . .)

WILD ABOUT 67!

Scientists have counted 67 species of mammals in Yellowstone National Park.

A band called Driver 67 had a hit song called "Car 67" in the United Kingdom in 1979.

67 **Ho**

Holmium is the chemical element with atomic number 67. It has the greatest magnetic strength of any element and is therefore used to make strong magnets.

68

SAY IT! WRITE IT!

English: sixty-eight

Spanish: sesenta y ocho

Mandarin: liùshíbā

Polish: sześćdziesiąt osiem

Roman: LXVIII

Chinese: 六十八

Mayan: :::

If you hiccupped 68 times, you might feel uncomfortable—but an Iowa man named Charles Osborne hiccupped for 68 straight years, from 1922 until 1990, when the hiccups suddenly stopped.

The total land and water area of Washington, DC, is approximately 68 square miles; 68 Leto is a large asteroid; 68 degrees Fahrenheit is exactly 20 degrees Celsius; and the maximum permitted length of a badminton racket is 68 centimeters.

DO THE MATH!

68 is **even**. $68 \div 2 = 34$

68 is **composite**.

Factors:
1, 2, 4, 17, 34, and 68

Tens	Ones
6	8

$68 = 2 \times 34 = 4 \times 17$

Prime Factorization:
$2 \times 2 \times 17$

68 is the sum of two squares: $64 + 4 = 68$, and of three squares: $36 + 16 + 16 = 68$.

SHOW ME 68!

$16 + 36 + 16 = 68$

$2 \times 2 \times 17 = 68$

WILD ABOUT 68!

The wingspan of a Boeing 747 is approximately 68 meters.

The NCAA Division I men's and women's basketball tournaments each begin with a total of 68 teams.

68 **Er**

Erbium is the chemical element with atomic number 68. Erbium is used in amplifiers, lasers, and photographic filters.

100
90
80
70
● 68
60
50
40
30
20
10
0

Up in space, M69 is the name of a globular cluster in the constellation Sagittarius that is estimated to contain about 125,000 stars. One degree of latitude on Earth's surface equals just over 69 miles. And if you rotate the numeral 69 upside down, it still looks like 69.

SAY IT! WRITE IT!

English: sixty-nine

Spanish: sesenta y nueve

Tagalog: animnapu't siyam

Russian: shest'desyat devyat'

Roman: LXIX

Babylonian: 𒐕 𒐏

Egyptian: ∩∩∩ ||| / ∩∩∩ |||

SHOW ME 69!

$3 \times 23 = 69$

$49 + 16 + 4 = 69$

DO THE MATH!

69 is **odd**.

69 is **composite**.

Factors: 1, 3, 23, and 69

Tens	Ones
6	9

Prime Factorization: 3×23

69 is the sum of three squares: $49 + 16 + 4 = 69$.

WILD ABOUT 69!

From 1983 until 2009, television channel numbers only went up to 69.

The symbol for the astrological sign Cancer sometimes looks like the number 69 sideways.

69
Tm

Thulium is the chemical element with atomic number 69. Thulium is also used in European paper money to discourage counterfeiting.

-100
-90
-80
69• -70
-60
-50
-40
-30
-20
-10
-0

70

The number 70 appears many times in the Bible. For example, the book of Genesis includes a list of the 70 descendants of Noah's sons, and in the book of Numbers, God asks Moses to bring him 70 elders of Israel. The traditional gift for a 70th wedding anniversary is something made of platinum (element 78). In 2019, David Rush set a world record by removing 70 socks from other people's feet in one minute while blindfolded.

DO THE MATH!

70 is **even**. $70 \div 2 = 35$

70 is **composite**.

Factors: 1, 2, 5, 7, 10, 14, 35, and 70

Tens	Ones
7	0

$70 = 2 \times 35 = 5 \times 14 = 7 \times 10$

Prime Factorization: $2 \times 5 \times 7$

70 is the sum of a square and a triangular number: $49 + 21 = 70$.

70 is the sum of three squares: $36 + 25 + 9 = 70$.

SHOW ME 70!

$2 \times 5 \times 7 = 70$

$49 + 21 = 70$

WILD ABOUT 70!

Queen Elizabeth II was the queen of England for over 70 years, from 1952 to 2022, making her the longest-serving monarch in English history.

At the Olympics, archery competitors shoot at a target 70 meters away.

70 Yb

Ytterbium is the chemical element with atomic number 70. Ytterbium is a bright, silvery rare earth metal that tarnishes quickly in air, which means it wouldn't be a good gift for a 70th wedding anniversary!

71

There were 71 judges on the Great Sanhedrin, the supreme court in ancient Israel. The Mexican Grand Prix, Brazilian Grand Prix, and Austrian Grand Prix are all car races that have exactly 71 laps. The traditional Bingo call for the number 71 is "Bang on the drum," which (sort of) rhymes with "seventy-one." And if you're ever at 71 Saint-Pierre Street in Quebec City, you can stay at Hotel 71!

SAY IT! WRITE IT!

English: seventy-one

Spanish: setenta y uno

French: soixante-et-onze (septante et un)

Hebrew: shiv'im ve achat

Roman: LXXI

Mayan: •••
⎯

Ancient Greek: οα

SHOW ME 71!

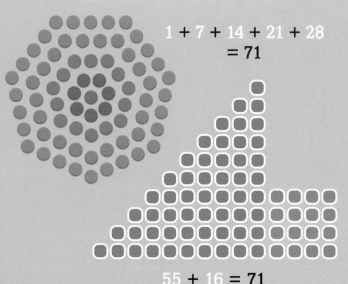

$1 + 7 + 14 + 21 + 28 = 71$

$55 + 16 = 71$

DO THE MATH!

71 is **odd**.

71 is **prime**.

Factors: 1 and 71

	Tens	Ones
	7	1

71 and 73 are twin primes.

71 is the sum of a triangular number and a square: $55 + 16 = 71$.

WILD ABOUT 71!

In the courtyard of the Louvre Museum in Paris, France, there is a glass pyramid that is 71 feet tall. It was designed by the famous architect I. M. Pei.

71 feet

About 71 percent of Earth's surface is covered by the ocean.

Lutetium is the chemical element with atomic number 71. Lutetium is used to find the age of meteorites.

72

SAY IT! WRITE IT!

English: seventy-two
Spanish: setenta y dos
Mandarin: qīshíèr
Vietnamese: bảy mươi hai

Roman: LXXII
Chinese: 七十二
Egyptian: ∩∩∩∩ ∩∩∩ II

Meet 72—also known as 6 dozen! In golf, most 18-hole courses have a total par of 72, and major golf tournaments have a total of 72 holes. King Louis XIV ruled France for 72 years—from 1643 to 1715—the longest verified reign of any king or queen in world history. In the tradition of Jewish mysticism called Kabbalah, there are 72 names of God. And in a famous scene in the movie *Rocky*, Sylvester Stallone runs up the 72 steps of the Philadelphia Museum of Art.

DO THE MATH!

72 is **even**. $72 \div 2 = 36$

72 is **composite**.

Factors: 1, 2, 3, 4, 6, 8, 9, 12, 18, 24, 36, and 72

Tens	Ones
7	2

$72 = 2 \times 36 = 3 \times 24 = 4 \times 18 = 6 \times 12 = 8 \times 9$

Prime Factorization:
$2 \times 2 \times 2 \times 3 \times 3$

72 is the difference of two squares: $81 - 9 = 72$.

72 is the sum of two cubes: $64 + 8 = 72$.

SHOW ME 72!

$8 \times 9 = 72$

$2 \times 2 \times 2 \times 3 \times 3 = 72$

$36 + 36 = 72$

●72

WILD ABOUT 72!

The American journalist Nellie Bly traveled around the world in just over 72 days, a record at the time. She was inspired by the novel *Around the World in Eighty Days*.

When Leonardo da Vinci wasn't painting or inventing, he was busy illustrating books by mathematicians. One polyhedron he drew had 72 faces and looked like this:

72
Hf

Hafnium is the chemical element with atomic number 72. Hafnium is used in nuclear reactors, light bulbs, flash bulbs, and computers.

73

If you like cats, you should know that the International Cat Association recognizes 73 breeds! Pizza 73 is a Canadian chain of pizza restaurants; in 2001, Barry Bonds of the San Francisco Giants hit 73 home runs in one season to set a Major League Baseball record; and there are 73 books in the Catholic Bible (46 in the Old Testament and 27 in the New Testament).

SAY IT! WRITE IT!

English: seventy-three

Spanish: setenta y tres

Arabic: thalatha wa-sab'un

Korean: ilheun set

Roman: LXXIII

Babylonian: 𒐖 𒐏𒐗

Thai: ๗๓

SHOW ME 73!

$1 + 12 + 24 + 36 = 73$

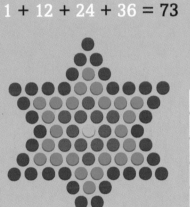

$45 + 28 = 73$

DO THE MATH!

73 is **odd**.

73 is **prime**.

Factors: 1 and 73

Tens	Ones
7	3

73 is the sum of two squares: $64 + 9 = 73$.

73 is the sum of two triangular numbers: $45 + 28 = 73$.

71 and 73 are the last twin primes we will meet in this book. (The next two twin primes are 101 and 103.)

WILD ABOUT 73!

73 in Morse code is a palindrome (the same backward as forward).

Hadrian's Wall runs for approximately 73 miles from coast to coast in Northern England. It was an ancient Roman fortification, and much of the wall still stands today.

73
Ta

Tantalum is the chemical element with atomic number 73. It has many uses, including in surgical equipment, artificial joints, capacitors, high-speed machine tools, and glass for camera lenses.

SAY IT! WRITE IT!

English: seventy-four

Spanish: setenta y cuatro

Yiddish: fir un zibetsik

Thai: chet sip si

Roman: LXXIV

Khmer: ៧៤

Cyrillic: ОД

You could say 74 is an important number for bears—black bears, brown bears, and polar bears have 74 chromosomes in their cells. Where else does 74 show up? The Whitsunday Islands—a popular tourist destination—are a group of 74 islands off the coast of Queensland, Australia. To be classified as a hurricane, a storm must have sustained winds of at least 74 miles per hour. And *Seventy-Four* is an orchestral composition by John Cage, written for 74 musicians.

DO THE MATH!

74 is **even**. 74 ÷ 2 = 37

74 is **composite**.

Factors:
1, 2, 37, and 74

Tens	Ones
7	4

Prime Factorization: 2 × 37

74 is the sum of two squares: 49 + 25 = 74.

74 is also the sum of three squares: 49 + 16 + 9 = 74.

SHOW ME 74!

49 + 25 = 74

2 × 37 = 74

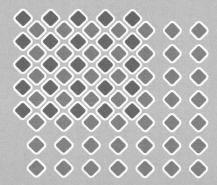

WILD ABOUT 74!

Wyoming Highway 74 is a very short highway: It is only about 230 yards long!

WYOMING 74

A *seventy-four* was a type of sailing ship used in the 18th and 19th centuries, so called because it had 74 cannons aboard.

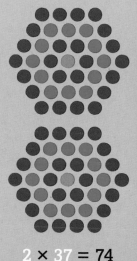

74 W

Tungsten is the chemical element with atomic number 74. Tungsten has the highest melting point of any metal. It is used for spacecraft parts that must withstand high temperatures.

100 — 90 — 80 — 74 — 70 — 60 — 50 — 40 — 30 — 20 — 10 — 0

75

You might have 75 in your pocket—if you have 3 quarters (or 15 nickels), you have 75 cents. Other facts about 75: Interstate 75 is a major north-south highway that travels from Florida to Michigan; we call a polygon with 75 sides a *heptacontapentagon*; and when you count to 75, you're three-fourths of the way to 100!

SAY IT! WRITE IT!

English: seventy-five

Spanish: setenta y cinco

Tagalog: pitumpu't lima

Haitian Creole: swasant kenz

Roman: LXXV

Mayan: ≡

Egyptian: ∩∩∩∩|||
∩∩∩ ||

SHOW ME 75!

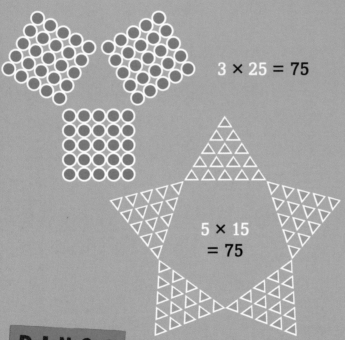

$3 \times 25 = 75$

$5 \times 15 = 75$

DO THE MATH!

75 is **odd**.

75 is **composite**.

Factors:
1, 3, 5, 15, 25, and 75

Tens	Ones
7	5

$75 = 3 \times 25 = 5 \times 15$

Prime Factorization:
$3 \times 5 \times 5$

75 is 3 times a square number: $3 \times 25 = 75$.

75 is 5 times a triangular number: $5 \times 15 = 75$.

75 is the difference of two squares: $100 - 25 = 75$.

BINGO

B	I	N	G	O
4	27	32	55	73
15	25	41	58	75
8	26	FREE	59	70
7	22	33	54	62
13	17	43	48	67

In Bingo, there are 75 balls numbered 1–75.

WILD ABOUT 75!

Twin and full mattresses are both 75 inches long.

75

Re

Rhenium is the chemical element with atomic number 75. It is used in flash lamps for photography, and in filaments for scientific instruments called mass spectrographs. Rhenium is also used in the production of unleaded gasoline.

76

The Philadelphia 76ers are an NBA basketball team. Their name commemorates the signing of the U.S. Declaration of Independence in Philadelphia in 1776. The song "Seventy-Six Trombones" was a popular song from the musical *The Music Man*. And if you multiply 76 × 76, you get 5,776—which ends with 76. And 5,776 × 76 = 438,976—which also ends with 76. This pattern continues. The only other two-digit number like this is 25.

DO THE MATH!

76 is **even**. 76 ÷ 2 = 38

76 is **composite**.

Factors:
1, 2, 4, 19, 38, and 76

Tens	Ones
7	6

76 = 2 × 38 = 4 × 19

Prime Factorization:
2 × 2 × 19

76 is the sum of two triangular numbers: 66 + 10 = 76.

76 is the sum of three squares: 36 + 36 + 4 = 76.

SHOW ME 76!

66 + 10 = 76

4 × 19 = 76

WILD ABOUT 76!

76 is the trademark of a chain of U.S. gas stations, whose "Spirit of 76" marketing campaigns celebrated the 1776 Declaration of Independence.

Halley's comet returns to the inner solar system (and is visible here on Earth) roughly every 76 years. Our next chance to see it will be in 2061!

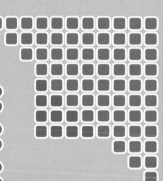

76
Os

Osmium is the chemical element with atomic number 76. An oxide of osmium gives off an unpleasant odor, so it is named for the Greek word *osme* (smell)—not for the Wizard of Oz.

77

Let's find out about 77—double sevens! The Rose Bowl stadium in Pasadena, California, has 77 rows of seats (and an official capacity of 92,542 people). The popular detective show *77 Sunset Strip* was on television from 1958 to 1964. And seventy-seven is the smallest whole number with a five-syllable name in English.

SHOW ME 77!

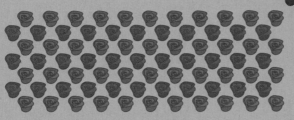

$7 \times 11 = 77$

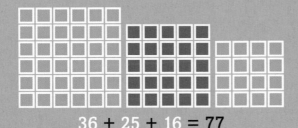

$36 + 25 + 16 = 77$

DO THE MATH!

77 is **odd**.

77 is **composite**.

Factors: 1, 7, 11, and 77

Tens	Ones
7	7

Prime Factorization: 7×11

77 is the difference of two squares: $81 - 4 = 77$.

77 is the sum of the first 8 prime numbers.

WILD ABOUT 77!

Scientists were recently surprised to discover 77 new animal species living on the seafloor under a 600-foot-thick ice shelf in Antarctica. The species included bryozoans (moss animals) and serpulid worms.

The Aston Martin One-77 was a very exclusive car manufactured from 2008–11. Only 77 were made, and they cost $2 million each!

77 Ir

Iridium is the chemical element with atomic number 77. Iridium is the most corrosion-resistant metal known. It is also the densest element. A piece the size of a soccer ball would weigh about 277 pounds!

100 — 90 — 80 — 77 • — 70 — 60 — 50 — 40 — 30 — 20 — 10 — 0

78

Each cell in a chicken has 39 pairs of gene-carrying chromosomes, for a total of $2 \times 39 = 78$ chromosomes. 78 is also the chromosome number in dogs, gray wolves, and coyotes. More about 78: Puerto Rico is divided into 78 municipalities; the length of an official tennis court is 78 feet; and in the song "The Twelve Days of Christmas," a total of 78 gifts are given on the twelfth day.

DO THE MATH!

78 is **even**. $78 \div 2 = 39$

78 is **composite**.

Factors: 1, 2, 3, 6, 13, 26, 39, and 78

Tens	Ones
7	8

$78 = 2 \times 39 = 3 \times 26 = 6 \times 13$

Prime Factorization: $2 \times 3 \times 13$

78 is a triangular number: $1 + 2 + 3 + \ldots + 11 + 12 = 78$.

78 is the sum of three squares: $49 + 25 + 4 = 78$.

SHOW ME 78!

$1 + 2 + 3 + 4 +$
$5 + 6 + 7 + 8 +$
$9 + 10 +$
$11 + 12$
$= 78$

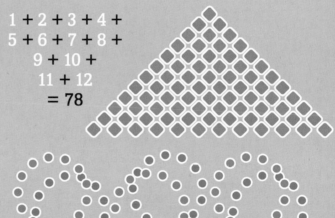

$2 \times 3 \times 13 = 78$

WILD ABOUT 78!

THE SUN

The earliest phonograph records usually played at a speed of 78 revolutions per minute. They were called "78s."

There are 78 cards in a standard deck of Tarot cards.

78 Pt

Platinum is the chemical element with atomic number 78. It is an extremely rare and valuable metal, often used in jewelry. In fact, the traditional gift for a 70th wedding anniversary is something made of platinum.

100
90
80
●78
70
60
50
40
30
20
10
0

79

The number 79 is called an *emirp* because 79 is prime, and if you reverse its digits, you get 97, which is also prime. (And "emirp" is "prime" backward.) A glacier in Greenland is called Nioghalvfjerdsbrae, which means 79 Glacier, because it's located at a latitude of 79 degrees north. And Interstate 79 is a highway that travels for about 343 miles from West Virginia to Pennsylvania.

SHOW ME 79!

$$64 + 15 = 79$$

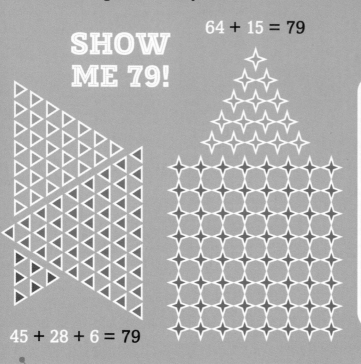

$$45 + 28 + 6 = 79$$

DO THE MATH!

79 is **odd**.

79 is **prime**.

Factors: 1 and 79

Tens	Ones
7	9

79 is the sum of a square and a triangular number: $64 + 15 = 79$.

79 and 83 are *cousin primes* (primes that differ by 4). Can you find other pairs of cousin primes?

WILD ABOUT 79!

The original *Star Trek* television series broadcast a total of 79 episodes.

79

Au

Gold is the chemical element with atomic number 79. Gold has been valued for thousands of years. The abbreviation *Au* comes from *aurum*, the Latin word for gold. Gold is the most malleable of all the elements, and commonly considered one of the most beautiful.

SAY IT! WRITE IT!

English: eighty

Spanish: ochenta

Mandarin: bāshí

Russian: vosem'desyat

Roman: LXXX

Chinese: 八十

Egyptian: ∩∩∩∩ ∩∩∩∩

To say "eighty," French speakers in France and Belgium generally say *quatre-vingts*, which means "four twenties." The word *octogenarian* is used to describe a person who is in their eighties. In the U.S. customary system of measurement, there are 80 chains in 1 mile (1 chain = 66 feet). *B.B. King & Friends: 80* was a record album by musician B. B. King released to celebrate his 80th birthday. And Eighty Mile Beach is a beach in Western Australia. Guess how long it is? About 137 miles!

DO THE MATH!

80 is **even**. 80 ÷ 2 = 40

80 is **composite**.

Factors: 1, 2, 4, 5, 8, 10, 16, 20, 40, and 80

Tens	Ones
8	0

80 = 2 × 40 = 4 × 20 = 5 × 16 = 8 × 10

Prime Factorization: 2 × 2 × 2 × 2 × 5

80 is the sum of two squares: 64 + 16 = 80.

80 is the sum of a triangular number and a square: 55 + 25 = 80.

SHOW ME 80!

2 × 2 × 2 × 2 × 5 = 80

WILD ABOUT 80!

Around the World in Eighty Days was a popular novel by the French author Jules Verne. The real-life journey of Nellie Bly (see entry under 72) was inspired by this novel.

80 Sappho is a large asteroid named for the Greek poet Sappho.

80
Hg

Mercury is the chemical element with atomic number 80. It is named for the planet Mercury, which in turn is named for the Roman god. Mercury is poisonous to humans if ingested.

100 —
90 —
80 — ● 80
70 —
60 —
50 —
40 —
30 —
20 —
10 —
0 —

81

The *Hare of Inaba* is a Japanese myth about 81 brothers and a hare. The youngest brother is kind to the hare, and he wins the heart of the princess over his brothers.

The number 81 is found elsewhere in the world, too! The country of Turkey is divided into 81 provinces. The *Tao Te Ching* is a classic Chinese text of 81 chapters composed over 2,000 years ago, and is one of the most translated texts in world literature. And in the United Kingdom, the traditional Bingo call for 81 is "Stop and Run."

SAY IT! WRITE IT!

English: eighty-one

Spanish: ochenta y uno

Tagalog: walumpu't isa

Arabic: wahid wa-thamanun

Roman: LXXXI

Babylonian: 𒐕 𒐏𒐕

Ancient Greek: πα

DO THE MATH!

81 is **odd**.

81 is **composite**.

Tens	Ones
8	1

Factors: 1, 3, 9, 27, and 81

$81 = 3 \times 27 = 9 \times 9$

Prime Factorization: $3 \times 3 \times 3 \times 3$

81 is a square number: $9 \times 9 = 81$.

81 is a 4th power: $3^4 = 3 \times 3 \times 3 \times 3 = 81$.

81 is the sum of two triangular numbers: $45 + 36 = 81$.

SHOW ME 81!

$3 \times 3 \times 3 \times 3 = 81$

$9 \times 9 = 81$

WILD ABOUT 81!

Sudoku is a Japanese number puzzle played on a 9 by 9 grid of 81 squares featuring a 3 by 3 arrangement of 3 by 3 squares. The player is given a partially filled grid, and the goal is to fill in each empty square with a digit from 1 to 9 so that each row, column, and 3 by 3 square contains all 9 digits.

5	3			7				
6			1	9	5			
	9	8					6	
8				6				3
4			8		3			1
7				2				6
	6					2	8	
			4	1	9			5
				8			7	9

The game of shogi, or Japanese chess, is played on a 9 by 9 grid with a total of 81 "squares" (which are often more rectangular—not quite square—in shape). Shogi pieces are shaped like pentagons.

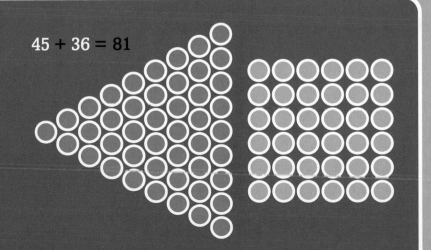

45 + 36 = 81

81

Tl

Thallium is the chemical element with atomic number 81. Thallium is highly toxic but can be used in photocells, infrared optical materials, and special types of glass.

82

In both the National Basketball Association and the National Hockey League, teams play a total of 82 games in the regular season. There are 82 ways to connect 6 regular hexagons together to make a figure called a *hexahex*. Erle Stanley Gardner wrote 82 novels featuring a defense lawyer named Perry Mason. And a standard dartboard is divided into 82 regions, including the bull's-eye in the center!

SHOW ME 82!

$2 \times 41 = 82$

$25 + 25 + 16 + 16 = 82$

DO THE MATH!

82 is **even**. $82 \div 2 = 41$

82 is **composite**.

Factors: 1, 2, 41, and 82

Tens	Ones
8	2

Prime Factorization: 2×41

82 is the sum of a triangular number and a square: $66 + 16 = 82$.

82 is the sum of two squares: $81 + 1 = 82$.

WILD ABOUT 82!

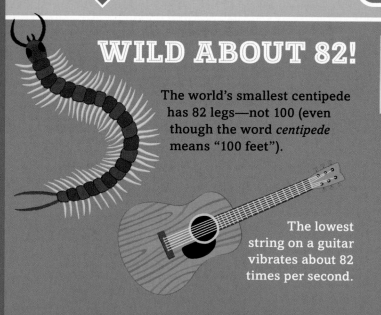

The world's smallest centipede has 82 legs—not 100 (even though the word *centipede* means "100 feet").

The lowest string on a guitar vibrates about 82 times per second.

82 **Pb**

Lead is the chemical element with atomic number 82. Lead has been used through the ages, including in plumbing by the ancient Romans, who didn't realize that it is a cumulative poison. Lead—in safe quantities—has many uses today, including in radiation shielding, roofing material, fine crystal, and storage batteries.

100 — 90 — 82● — 80 — 70 — 60 — 50 — 40 — 30 — 20 — 10 — 0

SAY IT! WRITE IT!

English: eighty-three

Spanish: ochenta y tres

Korean: yeodeun set

Hindi: tiraasee

Roman: LXXXIII

Chinese: 八十三

Mayan: ••••
⎯⎯
••••
•••

Meet 83, a proud, precious prime! Messier 83, a spiral galaxy also called the Southern Pinwheel galaxy, is about 15 million light-years away from Earth. Some Jewish men have a second bar mitzvah at age 83 to mark the passage of 70 years since their first bar mitzvah at age 13. The island nation of Vanuatu in the South Pacific Ocean contains (approximately) 83 islands.

DO THE MATH!

83 is **odd**.

83 is **prime**.

Factors:
1 and 83

Tens	Ones
8	3

83 is the sum of two triangular numbers: $55 + 28 = 83$.

83 is the sum of 5 consecutive primes: $11 + 13 + 17 + 19 + 23 = 83$.

SHOW ME 83!

$55 + 28 = 83$

$49 + 25 + 9 = 83$

WILD ABOUT 83!

83
Bi

Bismuth is the chemical element with atomic number 83. Bismuth oxide is used as a yellow pigment in paints and cosmetics.

Many people have trouble spelling the last name of English playwright William Shakespeare. In fact, a search of historical records found 83 different ways to spell it, including Shakysper, Schacosper, Shaxberd, and Shasspeere.

83 is the title of a 2021 Hindi-language film about India's victory in the 1983 Cricket World Cup.

84

Let's find out about 84! The town of Eighty Four in Pennsylvania was originally called Smithville, but its name was changed in 1884. In 7 dozens, there are 84 things, which means that 84 inches = 7 feet. And since 84 is the sum of the first 7 triangular numbers, it is a tetrahedral number. If you have 84 tennis balls, you can build a tetrahedron (or triangular pyramid) with triangular layers of 1, 3, 6, 10, 15, 21, and 28 balls.

SHOW ME 84!

$$2 \times 2 \times 3 \times 7 = 84$$

$$4 \times 21 = 84$$

DO THE MATH!

84 is **even**. $84 \div 2 = 42$

84 is **composite**.

Tens	Ones
8	4

Factors: 1, 2, 3, 4, 6, 7, 12, 14, 21, 28, 42, and 84

$84 = 2 \times 42 = 3 \times 28 = 4 \times 21 = 6 \times 14 = 7 \times 12$

Prime Factorization: $2 \times 2 \times 3 \times 7$

84 is the difference of two squares: $100 - 16 = 84$.

84 is the sum of two twin primes: $43 + 41 = 84$. Can you find other numbers like that?

WILD ABOUT 84!

A *snub dodecadodecahedron* is a polyhedron with 84 faces, including 60 triangles, 12 pentagons, and 12 pentagrams (stars).

84
Po

Polonium is the chemical element with atomic number 84. Polonium is a radioactive metalloid, the first element discovered by Marie Curie and Pierre Curie.

The planet Uranus takes 84 Earth years to orbit the Sun. If you lived on Uranus, it would be a long time between birthday parties!

85

Astronomers seem to like using 85—M85, NGC 85, 85 Ceti, 85 Pegasi, 85 Io, and 85D/Boethin are the names of various objects in space. Where else can we find 85? The Federalist Papers was a series of 85 articles and essays published in 1787 and 1788 to promote the ratification of the U.S. Constitution. And a hill in New Zealand is called Taumatawhakatangihangakoauauotamateaturipukakapikimaungahoronukupokaiwhenuakitanatahu—a name with 85 letters!

DO THE MATH!

85 is **odd**.

85 is **composite**.

Factors: 1, 5, 17, and 85

Tens	Ones
8	5

Prime Factorization: 5 × 17

85 is the sum of two squares in two different ways: 81 + 4 = 85 and 49 + 36 = 85.

SHOW ME 85!

49 + 36 = 85

5 × 17 = 85

WILD ABOUT 85!

85
At

Astatine is the chemical element with atomic number 85. It is the rarest naturally occurring element in Earth's crust; scientists estimate that only a few grams are present on Earth at any given time.

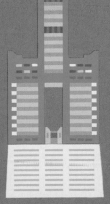

The 85 Sky Tower is an 85-story skyscraper in Asia.

In the 1990s two mathematicians proved that there are exactly 85 ways to tie a tie.

100

90

● 85

80

70

60

50

40

30

20

10

0

86

To *eighty-six* something is a slang phrase meaning to "get rid of it." Badwater Basin in Death Valley National Park, California, is 86 meters below sea level. It's the lowest point in the United States. And the 86th floor of the Empire State Building in New York City is where you'll find the main observation deck, though the building itself has 102 floors.

SAY IT! WRITE IT!

English: eighty-six

Spanish: ochenta y seis

Vietnamese: tám mươi sáu

Polish: osiemdziesiąt sześć

Roman: LXXXVI

Mayan: ⚫⚫⚫

Chinese Rod: ⊥ T

SHOW ME 86!

36 + 25 + 25 = 86

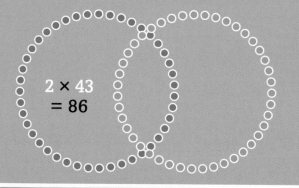

2 × 43 = 86

DO THE MATH!

86 is **even**. 86 ÷ 2 = 43

86 is **composite**.

Factors: 1, 2, 43, and 86

Tens	Ones
8	6

Prime Factorization: 2 × 43

86 is the sum of three squares: 36 + 25 + 25 = 86.

86 is also the sum of three triangular numbers: 55 + 21 + 10 = 86.

WILD ABOUT 86!

The first edition of *Grimm's Fairy Tales* contained 86 stories.

Agent 86 (Don Adams) was one of the main characters on *Get Smart*, a popular secret-agent TV comedy.

86
Rn

Radon is the chemical element with atomic number 86. Radon is highly radioactive and can be a hazard to human health.

SAY IT! WRITE IT!

English: eighty-seven

Spanish: ochenta y siete

Tagalog: walumpu't pito

Italian: ottantasette

Roman: LXXXVII

Chinese: 八十七

Hebrew: פז

The missing number in this puzzle is 87: 16, 06, 68, 88, __, 98. (Hint: look at it upside down!) The most popular model railway scale is 1:87, meaning that 1 inch on the model train represents 87 inches on a real train. Messier 87 is a supergiant elliptical galaxy in the constellation Virgo. It is a very large galaxy—much larger than our own Milky Way. And *decimoctoseptology* means the study of the number 87.

DO THE MATH!

87 is **odd**.

87 is **composite**.

Factors: 1, 3, 29, and 87

Tens	Ones
8	7

Prime Factorization: 3 × 29

87 is the sum of two triangular numbers: 66 + 21 = 87.

87 is the sum of the squares of the first 4 primes: 4 + 9 + 25 + 49 = 87.

SHOW ME 87!

$3 \times 29 = 87$

$66 + 21 = 87$

- 100
- 90
- ●87
- 80
- 70
- 60
- 50
- 40
- 30
- 20
- 10
- 0

WILD ABOUT 87!

Abraham Lincoln's famous speech, the Gettysburg Address, began like this: "Four score and seven years ago . . ." The year was 1863, and Lincoln was referring to the signing of the Declaration of Independence 87 years before. *Score* is a word for 20, so "four score and seven" means 4 × 20 + 7, or just 87.

A score of 87 in Australian cricket is considered very unlucky because it is 13 less than a century (100).

87

Fr

Francium is the chemical element with atomic number 87. Francium and astatine (element 85) were the last two naturally occurring elements to be discovered. Francium has no uses other than in scientific research.

Meet 88, another number that looks the same upside down as right side up! Since 8 is considered a lucky number in Chinese culture, so is 88. And in Chinese-language texts, 88 is a code that means "bye-bye" because the Mandarin for *eight-eight* is "bā-bā." The planet Mercury orbits the Sun once every 88 Earth days. And amateur radio operators use 88 as a code to mean "love and kisses"!

SHOW ME 88!

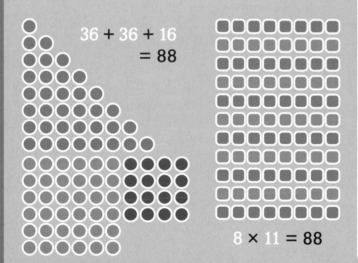

$$36 + 36 + 16 = 88$$

$$8 \times 11 = 88$$

DO THE MATH!

88 is **even**. $88 \div 2 = 44$

88 is **composite**.

Factors: 1, 2, 4, 8, 11, 22, 44, and 88

Tens	Ones
8	8

$88 = 2 \times 44 = 4 \times 22 = 8 \times 11$

Prime Factorization:
$2 \times 2 \times 2 \times 11$

88 is the sum of two triangular numbers: $78 + 10 = 88$.

88 is the sum of three squares: $36 + 36 + 16 = 88$.

WILD ABOUT 88!

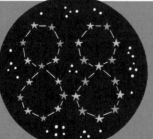

The International Astronomical Union recognizes 88 official constellations in the night sky.

88
Ra

Radium is the chemical element with atomic number 88. It was discovered by Marie Curie and Pierre Curie in 1898, a few months after they discovered polonium (element 84). Radium was once used in luminous paints for watches and clocks, but because of its dangerous radioactivity, now has only limited uses.

A standard piano keyboard has 88 keys.

Our galaxy has a large asteroid called 89 Julia—it is the "parent body" of the Julia family, a group of 33 asteroids that have similar orbits. The book of Numbers, Chapter 7, has 89 verses, the secondmost of any chapter in the Bible. U.S. Route 89 is a highway that runs from Arizona to the Canadian border, connecting seven national parks along the way. And Hellin's Law was a historical observation that twin births occurred approximately once in 89 births (which is no longer an accurate estimate).

SHOW ME 89!

$$64 + 25 = 89$$
$$4 \times 16 + 25 = 89$$

DO THE MATH!

89 is odd.

89 is prime.

Factors: 1 and 89

Tens	Ones
8	9

89 is the sum of two squares: $64 + 25 = 89$.

WILD ABOUT 89!

Butterflies like this are found in South America. The markings on its wings look like 89!

The seeds on sunflowers are often arranged in 89 counterclockwise spirals.

89
Ac

Actinium is the chemical element with atomic number 89. It is highly radioactive and has no significant commercial uses. However, actinium has been used by scientists to study the way the water at different ocean depths mixes over time, a process sometimes called deep-sea mixing.

● 89

100
90
80
70
60
50
40
30
20
10
0

In the United Kingdom, there are 90 numbers in the game of Bingo (instead of 75 as in the United States). The traditional Bingo calls for the number 90 are "Top of the Shop" or "End of the Line." In geometry, an angle that measures 90 degrees is called a *right angle*. If you're at a latitude of 90 degrees north, you're at the North Pole. If you're at a latitude of 90 degrees south, you're at the South Pole. And a game of soccer lasts for 90 minutes.

SHOW ME 90!

$$45 + 45 = 90$$
$$9 \times 10 = 90$$

$$2 \times 3 \times 3 \times 5 = 90$$

DO THE MATH!

90 is **even**. $90 \div 2 = 45$

90 is **composite**.

Factors:
1, 2, 3, 5, 6, 9, 10, 15, 18, 30, 45, and 90

Tens	Ones
9	0

$90 = 2 \times 45 = 3 \times 30 = 5 \times 18 = 6 \times 15 = 9 \times 10$

Prime Factorization:
$2 \times 3 \times 3 \times 5$

90 is the sum of two squares: $81 + 9 = 90$.

90 is the sum of 6 consecutive prime numbers: $7 + 11 + 13 + 17 + 19 + 23 = 90$.

WILD ABOUT 90!

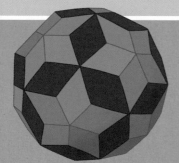

A *rhombic enneacontahedron* is a polyhedron with 90 faces: 60 wide rhombuses and 30 narrow rhombuses.

In baseball, the bases are 90 feet apart.

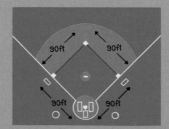

90 Th

Thorium is the chemical element with atomic number 90. Thorium is named for Thor, the Norse god of thunder. Thorium has many uses, including in lantern mantles, ceramics, glass, and light bulbs.

SAY IT! WRITE IT!

English: ninety-one

Spanish: noventa y uno

Russian: devyanosto odin

Gujarati: ekāṇuñ

Roman: XCI

Mayan: ≐

Cyrillic: ЧА

If you have 91 oranges, you're in luck—you can build a square pyramid with layers of 1, 4, 9, 16, 25, and 36 oranges. We say that 91 is a square pyramidal number. A period of 91 days (or 13 weeks, since 13 × 7 = 91) is approximately one-fourth of a year, or three months. Ninety-One is a solitaire card game where the goal is to move cards onto piles so that the top cards add up to 91. STS-91 was a mission flown by space shuttle *Discovery* to the *Mir* space station. And if you have 1 penny, 1 nickel, 1 dime, 1 quarter, and 1 half-dollar coin, you have 91 cents!

DO THE MATH!

91 is **odd**.

91 is **composite**.

Factors:
1, 7, 13, and 91

Tens	Ones
9	1

Prime Factorization:
7 × 13

91 is a triangular number:
1 + 2 + 3 + . . . + 12 + 13 = 91.

91 is a centered hexagonal number:
1 + 6 + 12 + 18 + 24 + 30 = 91.

SHOW ME 91!

1 + 6 + 12 + 18 + 24 + 30 = **91**

WILD ABOUT 91!

There are 91 species of mammals that are known to live in Grand Canyon National Park, including mountain lions, bighorn sheep, and hog-nosed skunks.

The temple of Kukulcán (often called El Castillo) is an ancient Mayan step-pyramid. There are 91 steps climbing up each triangular face.

91
Pa

Protactinium is the chemical element with atomic number 91. Because it is rare, expensive to produce, toxic, and radioactive, it has no uses outside of basic scientific research.

100 —

90 — ● 91

80 —

70 —

60 —

50 —

40 —

30 —

20 —

10 —

0 —

92

Where can we find 92? In geometry, a *snub dodecahedron* is a polyhedron with 92 faces. In the game of chess, there are 92 solutions to the *eight queens puzzle*, which is the problem of placing 8 chess queens on an 8 by 8 chessboard so that no two queens are attacking each other. And 92 Moose is a radio station that broadcasts at 92.3 MHz from Augusta, Maine.

SAY IT! WRITE IT!

English: ninety-two

Spanish: noventa y dos

Mandarin: jiǔshíèr

Portuguese: noventa e dois

Roman: XCII

Ancient Greek: ϙβ

Chinese: 九十二

SHOW ME 92!

$49 + 25 + 9 + 9 = 92$

$64 + 28 = 92$

DO THE MATH!

92 is **even**. $92 \div 2 = 46$

92 is **composite**.

Factors:
1, 2, 4, 23, 46, and 92

Tens	Ones
9	2

$92 = 2 \times 46 = 4 \times 23$

Prime Factorization:
$2 \times 2 \times 23$

92 is the sum of a square and a triangular number: $64 + 28 = 92$.

92 is the sum of three cubes: $64 + 27 + 1 = 92$.

WILD ABOUT 92!

Johnny Cash's recording of "I've Been Everywhere" lists 92 places the singer had visited in North America. The song was written by singer Geoff Mack, whose original version lists 94 places in Australia.

92
U

Uranium is the chemical element with atomic number 92. The French scientist Henri Becquerel was experimenting with uranium when he discovered radioactivity. Uranium is widely used as a source of energy in nuclear power reactors.

92 is the greatest number of pieces into which you could cut a pizza with 13 straight cuts.

SAY IT! WRITE IT!

English: ninety-three

Spanish: noventa y tres

Tagalog: siyamnapu't tatlo

Vietnamese: chín mươi ba

Roman: XCIII

Babylonian: 𒐕 𒌋𒌋𒌋

Thai: ๙๓

You can find 93 in space: 93 Minerva is a large asteroid named after the Roman goddess of wisdom. It has a diameter of about 150 kilometers, and it has two small moons of its own. And the average distance from Earth to the Sun is about 93 million miles, a distance also known as 1 astronomical unit.

SHOW ME 93!

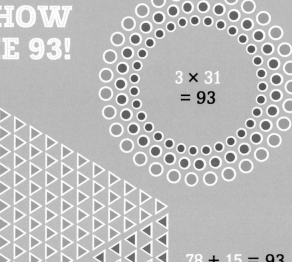

$3 \times 31 = 93$

$78 + 15 = 93$

DO THE MATH!

93 is **odd**.

93 is **composite**.

Factors: 1, 3, 31, and 93

Tens	Ones
9	3

Prime Factorization: 3×31

93 is the sum of three squares: $64 + 25 + 4 = 93$.

93 is the sum of two triangular numbers: $78 + 15 = 93$.

WILD ABOUT 93!

93 is the greatest number of pieces you could cut a cake into with eight straight cuts (including horizontally).

From the ground to the top of its torch, the Statue of Liberty measures 93 meters tall.

93
Np

Neptunium is the chemical element with atomic number 93. Neptunium is used in neutron detectors and to help with the production of plutonium.

●93

100 —
90 —
80 —
70 —
60 —
50 —
40 —
30 —
20 —
10 —
0 —

Interstate 94 is a major east-west highway that travels from Montana to Michigan. Along the way, I-94 passes through Chicago, where Hustle Chicago is a stair-climbing race up 94 floors of a skyscraper. The record time is less than 10 minutes! The baseball player Babe Ruth was famous for hitting 714 home runs, but did you know that he also won 94 games as a pitcher?

SHOW ME 94!

$66 + 28 = 94$

$49 + 36 + 9 = 94$

DO THE MATH!

94 is **even**. $94 \div 2 = 47$

94 is **composite**.

Factors: 1, 2, 47, and 94

Tens	Ones
9	4

Prime Factorization: 2×47

94 is the sum of three squares: $49 + 36 + 9 = 94$.

94 is the sum of two triangular numbers: $66 + 28 = 94$.

WILD ABOUT 94!

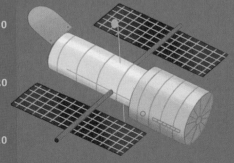

The main mirror of the Hubble Space Telescope has a diameter of 94.5 inches.

An NBA basketball court is 94 feet long.

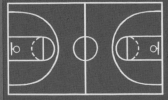

94
Pu

Plutonium is the chemical element with atomic number 94. It is named for the dwarf planet Pluto. Plutonium is used in nuclear power reactors, and to provide power for space probes that travel too far from the Sun to use solar power.

95

SAY IT! WRITE IT!

English: ninety-five

Spanish: noventa y cinco

French: quatre-vingt-quinze (nonante-cinq)

Hawaiian: kanaiwakūmālima

Roman: XCV

Chinese: 九十五

Bengali: ৯৫

Here are some interesting facts about 95: Many followers of the Bahá'í faith make a daily practice of repeating the prayer *Alláh-u-Abhá* (God is most glorious) 95 times. In the 2006 film *Cars*, 95 is Lightning McQueen's number. And in statistics, if you're 95 percent certain about something, that's considered good enough for most purposes.

DO THE MATH!

95 is **odd**.

95 is **composite**.

Factors:
1, 5, 19, and 95

Tens	Ones
9	5

Prime Factorization: 5 × 19

95 is the sum of four squares: 36 + 25 + 25 + 9 = 95.

SHOW ME 95!

45 + 25 + 25 = 95

17 + 18 + 19 + 20 + 21 = 95

WILD ABOUT 95!

The "Ninety-Five Theses" is a list of 95 discussion points about Catholicism written in 1517 by Martin Luther. Its publication is considered to be the start of the Protestant Reformation.

The state of Tennessee has 95 counties.

95
Am

Americium is the chemical element with atomic number 95. It is used in smoke detectors and as a portable source of gamma rays and alpha particles for use in medicine and in scientific research.

96

Ishido: The Way of Stones is a puzzle video game that is played on a gameboard of 96 squares arranged in an 8 by 12 rectangle. The ancient Greek mathematician Archimedes found a very accurate approximation of pi (the ratio of a circle's circumference to its diameter, approximately 3.141592) using a regular polygon with 96 sides (an *enneacontahexagon*). And the first artificial satellite, Sputnik 1, orbited Earth once every 96 minutes.

SHOW ME 96!

16 + 64 + 16 = 96

$2 \times 2 \times 2 \times 2 \times 2 \times 3 = 96$

$6 \times 16 = 96$

DO THE MATH!

96 is **even**. $96 \div 2 = 48$

96 is **composite**.

Factors:
1, 2, 3, 4, 6, 8, 12, 16, 24, 32, 48, and 96

Tens	Ones
9	6

$96 = 2 \times 48 = 3 \times 32 = 4 \times 24 = 6 \times 16 = 8 \times 12$

Prime Factorization:
$2 \times 2 \times 2 \times 2 \times 2 \times 3$

96 is the sum of three squares: $64 + 16 + 16 = 96$.

96 is the difference of two squares: $100 - 4 = 96$.

WILD ABOUT 96!

The 96-crayon box is one of the popular choices offered by Crayola.

Ninety Six is a town in South Carolina. A boy from Ninety Six named Bill Voiselle grew up to play major-league baseball, and he wore the uniform number 96 in honor of his hometown.

96 Cm

Curium is the chemical element with atomic number 96. Curium was first synthesized in 1944, and it is named for Marie and Pierre Curie, who were pioneers in early research on radioactive elements.

SAY IT! WRITE IT!

English: ninety-seven

Spanish: noventa y siete

Khmer: kao sep pram pii

Yiddish: zibn un nayntsik

Roman: XCVII

Babylonian: 𒐕 𒐏𒐏𒐖

Devanagari: ९७

A polygon with 97 sides is called an *enneacontaheptagon*! In the Gregorian calendar used in most of the world, there are 97 leap years in every 400-year cycle. Messier 97, also called the Owl Nebula, is a planetary nebula in the constellation Ursa Major (often called the Big Dipper). And Lehigh University's marching band is called the "Marching 97" because it has 97 members!

DO THE MATH!

97 is **odd**.

97 is **prime**.

Factors:
1 and 97

Tens	Ones
9	7

97 is the sum of two squares: $81 + 16 = 97$.

97 is also the sum of three squares: $36 + 36 + 25 = 97$.

SHOW ME 97!

$$36 + 25 + 36 = 97$$

WILD ABOUT 97!

In 1956, Yankees pitcher Don Larsen threw the only perfect game in World Series history; he threw a total of 97 pitches and retired 27 batters in a row.

97 Bk

Berkelium is the chemical element with atomic number 97. It was discovered in the 1940s in Berkeley, California.

Hot 97 is a radio station in New York City that broadcasts at 97.1 FM.

100 — ● 97
90 —
80 —
70 —
60 —
50 —
40 —
30 —
20 —
10 —
0 —

98

Expo '98 was a World's Fair held in Portugal in 1998. It received more than 10 million visitors over a period of four months. Denmark is divided into five regions that contain a total of 98 municipalities. STS-98 was a 2001 mission to the International Space Station flown by space shuttle *Atlantis*. And 98 Degrees is an American band that has sold over 10 million records.

SHOW ME 98!

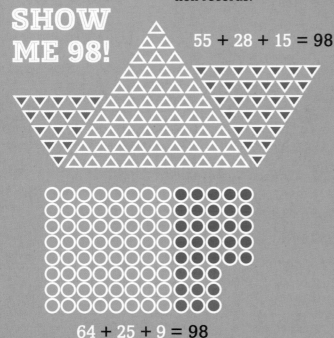

$55 + 28 + 15 = 98$

$64 + 25 + 9 = 98$

DO THE MATH!

98 is **even**. $98 \div 2 = 49$

98 is **composite**.

Factors: 1, 2, 7, 14, 49, and 98

Tens	Ones
9	8

$98 = 2 \times 49 = 7 \times 14$

Prime Factorization: $2 \times 7 \times 7$

98 is twice a square: $2 \times 49 = 98$.

98 is also the sum of three squares: $64 + 25 + 9 = 98$.

WILD ABOUT 98!

98 is the highest jersey number allowed in the National Hockey League, because only one- and two-digit numbers are allowed, and the number 99 has been retired in honor of Wayne Gretzky ("the Great One").

There are 98 wooden covered bridges in the state of Indiana.

98 Cf

Californium is the chemical element with atomic number 98. It was first produced in 1950 in Berkeley, California (and the name "berkelium" was already taken).

English: ninety-nine

Spanish: noventa y nueve

Tagalog: siyamnapu't siyam

Serbo-Croatian: devedeset devet

Roman: XCIX

Ancient Greek: ϙθ

Egyptian: ∩∩∩||| ∩∩∩||| ∩∩∩|||

In the tradition of Islam there are 99 names for Allah (God), including "The Creator," "The Most Loving," and "The Giver of Gifts." Agent 99 (Barbara Feldon) was one of the main characters on *Get Smart*, a popular secret-agent TV comedy. And many items have prices that end in .99, but don't be fooled—a price of $2.99 basically means 3 bucks!

DO THE MATH!

99 is **odd**.

99 is **composite**.

Factors:
1, 3, 9, 11, 33, and 99

Tens	Ones
9	9

$99 = 3 \times 33 = 9 \times 11$

Prime Factorization:
$3 \times 3 \times 11$

99 is the sum of three squares: $25 + 25 + 49 = 99$.

99 is also the sum of three cubes: $64 + 27 + 8 = 99$.

SHOW ME 99!

$3 \times 3 \times 11 = 99$

$25 + 49 + 25 = 99$

WILD ABOUT 99!

It took 99 days for a team led by the British explorer Sir Vivian Fuchs to cross Antarctica in 1957–1958. This was the first overland crossing of Antarctica via the South Pole. The plan was to make the journey in 100 days, but they finished 1 day ahead of schedule!

The Ninety-Nines: International Organization of Women Pilots was founded in 1929 by a group of 99 women pilots. The group's first president was Amelia Earhart.

99
Es

Einsteinium is the chemical element with atomic number 99. It is named for the famous physicist Albert Einstein.

100

100● 100

SAY IT! WRITE IT!

English: one hundred
Spanish: cien
Mandarin: yībǎi
Italian: cento

Roman: C
Babylonian:
Chinese: 一百

Welcome to 100, the last number in this book and the only one with three digits! The Latin word for 100 is *centum*. From this comes the root word *cent* and the prefix *centi-*, which appear in many English words meaning either a hundred or one-hundredth. Examples include **cent**ury, **cent**enarian, **centi**meter, **centi**pede, and **cent**ennial. The insects called **centi**pedes have lots of legs, anywhere from 30 to 382—but no centipede species has exactly 100 legs.

The *Kármán line* is an altitude of 100 kilometers above the surface of Earth. This is generally considered to be the boundary between Earth's atmosphere and outer space. There are 100 senators in the United States Senate, 2 senators from each of the 50 states. On the Celsius temperature scale, water boils at 100 degrees and freezes at 0 degrees. The Celsius temperature scale is also called the *centigrade* scale.

In mathematics, 100 is the basis for per**cent**s. Having 100 percent of something means all of it, 50 percent of something means half of it, and 1 percent of something means one-hundredth of it. And if you multiply 10 by itself 100 times (which you could write with an exponent, like this: 10^{100}), you get a very large number called a *googol*. It's a 1 followed by 100 zeros!

DO THE MATH!

100 is **even**. $100 \div 2 = 50$

100 is **composite**.

Hundreds	Tens	Ones
1	0	0

Factors: 1, 2, 4, 5, 10, 20, 25, 50, and 100

$100 = 2 \times 50 = 4 \times 25 = 5 \times 20 = 10 \times 10$

Prime Factorization: $2 \times 2 \times 5 \times 5$

100 is a square number: $10^2 = 10 \times 10 = 100$.

Like all square numbers, 100 is the sum of two consecutive triangular numbers: $45 + 55 = 100$.

100 is also the sum of two squares: $64 + 36 = 100$.

100 is the sum of the first nine prime numbers (from 2 to 23).

100 is the sum of the first four cubes: $1 + 8 + 27 + 64 = 100$.

WILD ABOUT 100!

In American football, the field is 100 yards in length, not including the end zones.

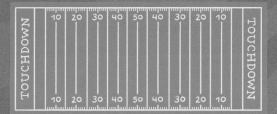

The $100 bill is the largest denomination currently printed in the United States. It features a picture of Benjamin Franklin, so some people call $100 bills "Bens."

On the Jewish holiday of Rosh Hashanah, a musical horn called a *shofar* is typically blown 100 times.

The 100-meter dash is one of the most celebrated track-and-field events.

100 **Fm**

Fermium is the chemical element with atomic number 100. It is named after the Italian physicist Enrico Fermi.

SHOW ME 100!

55 + 45 = 100

2 × 2 × 5 × 5 = 100

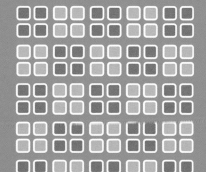

10 × 10 = 100
4 × 25 = 100

GLOSSARY

composite A number is *composite* if it has factors other than 1 and the number itself. For example, 20 is composite because its factors are 1, 2, 4, 5, 10, and 20. Any number (other than 1) that is **not** prime is composite.

counting numbers (or **natural numbers**) The *counting numbers* are the numbers {1, 2, 3, 4, 5, . . .}. The counting numbers continue forever. They are also called the *natural numbers*.

difference When you subtract two numbers, the resulting number is called the *difference*.

divisible One number is *divisible* by another number if it divides evenly into the number without a remainder. For example, 20 is divisible by 5 because $20 \div 5 = 4$.

divisor A *divisor* is a number that can be divided evenly into another number. For example, 5 is a divisor of 20 because $20 \div 5 = 4$.

even A number is *even* if it can be divided evenly by 2 without a remainder. For example, 28 is even because $28 \div 2 = 14$.

factor *Factors* are numbers that can be multiplied to get a certain number. For example, 4 and 5 are factors of 20 because $4 \times 5 = 20$. Factors and divisors are the same thing.

Fibonacci number The *Fibonacci numbers* are the numbers in the following sequence: {1, 1, 2, 3, 5, 8, 13, 21, 34, 55, 89, . . .}. After the first two 1s, each number in the Fibonacci sequence is the sum of the two previous numbers.

multiple A *multiple* of a number is the result of multiplying it by a counting number. For example, 15 is a multiple of 3 because $3 \times 5 = 15$. The *multiples* of 3 are 3, 6, 9, 12, 15, 18, and so on.

odd A number is *odd* if it **cannot** be divided evenly by 2 without a remainder. For example, 29 is odd because $29 \div 2 = 14$ R1 (remainder 1).

prime A number is *prime* if its only factors are 1 and the number itself. For example, 17 is prime because 1 and 17 are its only factors. In other words, 17 is divisible only by 1 and 17. The first few prime numbers are 2, 3, 5, 7, 11, 13, 17, 19, and 23.

prime factorization The *prime factorization* of a number shows the number written as a product of prime factors. For example, the prime factorization of 20 is 2 × 2 × 5. Each counting number has only one prime factorization.

square number A *square number* (or just a *square*) is a number that results from multiplying a counting number by itself. For example, 16 is a square because 16 = 4 × 4. The square numbers are 1, 4, 9, 16, 25, 36, and so on. If you have a square number of shapes, you can arrange them to make a square, as shown:

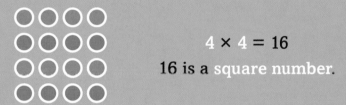

4 × 4 = 16

16 is a square number.

sum When you add two or more numbers, the resulting total is called the *sum*.

triangular number A *triangular number* is the result of adding 1 + 2 + . . . + N. For example, 6 is a triangular number because 1 + 2 + 3 = 6. The triangular numbers are 1, 3, 6, 10, 15, 21, and so on. If you have a triangular number of shapes, you can arrange them to make a triangle, as shown:

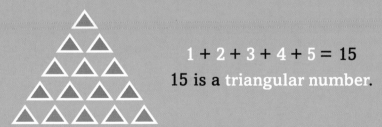

1 + 2 + 3 + 4 + 5 = 15

15 is a triangular number.

twin primes Two prime numbers are called *twin primes* if they differ by 2. For example, 17 and 19 are twin primes.

whole numbers The *whole numbers* are the counting numbers, plus zero: {0, 1, 2, 3, 4, 5, . . .}.

THE MULTIPLICATION TABLE

Here's a table with all the basic multiplication facts up to 12 × 12. Of course, you can always draw and count dots to help you figure out a multiplication question, but it's much easier if you can memorize the answer or use a table like this to help!

For example, to solve 5 × 8, look for 5 in the column on the left and 8 in the top row, then find the number where they meet: 40. Cool!

This table can also be used for division. To solve 27 ÷ 3, for example, find 27 in the "**3**" row and move straight up to discover your quotient: 9.

x	1	2	3	4	5	6	7	8	9	10	11	12
1	1	2	3	4	5	6	7	8	9	10	11	12
2	2	4	6	8	10	12	14	16	18	20	22	24
3	3	6	9	12	15	18	21	24	27	30	33	36
4	4	8	12	16	20	24	28	32	36	40	44	48
5	5	10	15	20	25	30	35	40	45	50	55	60
6	6	12	18	24	30	36	42	48	54	60	66	72
7	7	14	21	28	35	42	49	56	63	70	77	84
8	8	16	24	32	40	48	56	64	72	80	88	96
9	9	18	27	36	45	54	63	72	81	90	99	108
10	10	20	30	40	50	60	70	80	90	100	110	120
11	11	22	33	44	55	66	77	88	99	110	121	132
12	12	24	36	48	60	72	84	96	108	120	132	144